the secret language of
love

the secret language of
love

a visual treasury of love through the ages

MEGAN TRESIDDER

with paintings by Emma Turpin

CHRONICLE BOOKS
SAN FRANCISCO

First published in the United States in 2004 by Chronicle Books LLC.

Copyright © 1997, 2004 by Duncan Baird Publishers
Text copyright © 1997, 2004 by Megan Tresidder estate
Illustrations and commissioned photographs copyright © 1997, 2004 by Duncan Baird Publishers

Paintings reproduced on pages 2, 5, 8, 18, 31, 39, 45, 50, 56, 76–7, 82, 85, 102, 118, 139, 153, 163, 169 © Emma Turpin
For copyright of photographs, see page 176, which is to be regarded as an extension of this copyright. All rights reserved. No part of this book may be reproduced in any form without the prior written permission of the Publisher.

Editor: Joanne Clay
Designer: Gail Jones
Picture Research: Julia Brown
Cover Design: Benjamin Shaykin

Library of Congress Cataloguing-in-Publication Data:

Tresidder, Megan, 1958–2001
The secret language of love / by Megan Tresidder.
p. cm.
Includes bibliographical referencec and index.
ISBN 0-8118-4151-0
1. Love. I. Title.
HO 801. T765   1997
306.7—dc20 96-10958
CIP

Typeset in Mrs Eaves
Font designed by Zuzana Licko
Manufactured in Thailand

Distributed in Canada by
Raincoast Books
9050 Shaughnessy Street
Vancouver, B.C. V6P 6E5

10 9 8 7 6 5 4 3 2 1

Chronicle Books LLC
85 Second Street
San Francisco, CA 94105
www.chroniclebooks.com

CONTENTS

Contents

INTRODUCTION

O love is the crooked thing,
There is nobody wise enough
To find out all that is in it.
W. B. YEATS (1865–1939), "BROWN PENNY"

Love is the most complex and important of all human emotions. It defies adequate definition, but in its grandeur and its imaginative power over our lives, it can be both creative and destructive, beautiful and terrifying.

Love is more than simply affection, although the same word is increasingly used for both emotions. It has many mysteries and many faces. An ascetic's yearning for the spirit of God or for an Absolute, the love between parents and children or brothers and sisters, the bond between two loving friends, the enduring contentment between a loving couple long after sexual desire has ebbed, are all forms of deep love – some would say stronger and

Introduction

more permanent than romantic passion. To understand love, we need to look at all of these forms and at the mysterious connections and overlaps between them. However, at the core of this book, as at the centre of the human imagination, is erotic love.

From one point of view, all forms of true love are erotic if they involve longing. The Greek *eros*, or "passion-love", is the unmistakably sexual desire to fuse with what we sense is missing. Such love renews itself with every generation, despite numerous texts which document its often tragic consequences. Unhappy love, frustrated love, doomed love or lost love are dominant themes in the novel, drama, classical ballet, opera and cinema. Religion, philosophy and psychology often seem to distrust the irresponsible wildness of passionate love, placing a higher value on more temperate personal relationships or on a more diffused love for humankind, or for God.

Yet it is not difficult to see why passionate love has such a compelling attraction. It fascinates us because it promises a happiness that is not temperate but extraordinary. Under the influence of love the world around us looks completely different. The mundane burdens of everyday life seem to be infinitely lighter. The sight and touch of the Other intoxicates us, and the thought of returning alone to an ordinary world is almost unbearable.

This book reviews some of the most significant ideas people have had about the nature of love, and identifies the fundamental archetypes that unconsciously influence our behaviour. It discusses the many facets of love and the ever-changing language of flirtation, courtship and fulfilment. Above all, it celebrates love as erotic, passionate and romantic, as a magical transformation.

Modern love has grown out of a bewildering mixture of rituals, fashions, laws and customs. Philosophical theories

Introduction

Introduction

Weddings in the 19th century followed an often long and formal period of courtship. This illustration from *La mode illustrée* shows a bride having a dress fitting.

and religious prohibitions or commandments have also contributed, as have literary role models. Compared with almost any other period in history, love has never been so liberated from social restrictions as it is now.

This does not mean that it is any easier to fall in love or to sustain romantic passion today. The opposite may be true. The history of love has shown repeatedly that longing is positively increased by obstacles and delays, separations and rules of courtship. The steady removal of these rules has profoundly changed the nature of human relationships in the Western world.

Throughout the ages there has been fundamental disagreement not only about what makes us fall in love but also about whether the romantic concept of falling in love is "real love" at all. Another form of love has traditionally been placed higher in the moral scale. The

Greeks called it *agape*, love for humankind. It is often linked with the ideal of Christian love because it looks beyond our own desires or needs toward the requirements of others.

The nobility of this form of love is indisputable. It coincides with what Christians see as the "gift love" of God, and involves a conscious act of free will, a choice. Passionate love, on the other hand, seems to offer us no choice at all. It simply overwhelms us, welling up as an unconscious or instinctive force which we are powerless to resist. Eros was the Greek personification of this force.

The sexual content of *eros* has always been distrusted by philosophers, and is still distrusted by psychotherapists who have to deal with the problems that it creates. At times in the history of love, a rigid division has been drawn

The concept of courtly love, in which a lover surrendered his heart to his lady, first flourished in medieval France. Its influence survives today in many myths and romances. In this 16th-century tapestry, a suitor reads a love poem to his lady in a symbolic garden setting.

Introduction

between *eros* and *agape*, as if sexual and selfless love could never be combined. In late medieval Europe, the Church looked to the teachings of St Paul which were founded upon a distinction between spiritual and physical union. This anti-erotic view gave little encouragement in scripture to secular love; virginity and chastity were praised above marriage.

Although most world philosophies acknowledge that love is a multi-faceted emotion, Eastern religions have long recognized that love can play an important role in spiritual happiness. Highly erotic carvings, such as depictions of the sexual exploits of Krishna and the *gopi* (milkmaid) Radha, decorate the façades of some Hindu temples, while the sexual and spiritual union of Shiva and Parvati became the basis of Tantric and Shakta philosophy.

In a period of new humanism, artists and writers of the European Renaissance swept away the idea that sexual love was inconsistent with sacred love. They

In this 15th-century Italian painting, the triumph of the goddess Venus is being venerated by six legendary lovers: Achilles, Tristan, Lancelot, Samson, Paris and Troilus.

described love between men and women as a joyous and transforming emotion, which in turn celebrated a divine, natural authority. Most modern writers on love believe that *eros* and *agape* are not only reconcilable, but that one can grow out of the other. Romantic love can develop into the loving friendship of mature love, still carrying the charge of passion that inspired it.

History shows that passionate love is a prize that is not easily won. At its heart is the risk of error, disappointment or torment. Young lovers take the greatest risks of love not lasting because for

Titian's *Sacred and Profane Love*, painted around 1515, is an ironic portrayal of the medieval belief that secular love is a second-rate emotion. The artist depicted the divine Venus naked, the earthly one clothed, recognizing the erotic potential in concealment.

Introduction

The story of the Hindu god Krishna and the *gopi* (milkmaid) Radha is one of the greatest Indian romances. This painting depicts Krishna walking in a grove with his beloved Radha. In the bottom left, she tenderly anoints her lover's feet.

them, falling in love is often part of the whole process of self-discovery. The idea of possessing the loved one comes later, and the risk of loss is then even more painful, unless the lovers can move beyond self. Selfishness is always a component of falling in love. We want to adore another person, but we also want to be adored ourselves. Not to have our love reciprocated is anguish enough. Being loved and then losing that love is agonizing. It is love's mingling of joy and sorrow that will continue to haunt the human imagination.

In Western societies, many of the old restrictions and rigid codes of conduct were designed to protect women against giving birth to children outside the security of a "suitable" marriage. In changing the pattern of sexual relationships, safe contraception has altered patterns of love as well. For example, courtship rules meant that lovers seldom had to sustain intimate

Introduction

relationships with each other before they were married. And after marriage, an interplay of separation and intimacy was imposed by clear distinctions between male and female roles in society. A degree of mystery was maintained between the sexes. Nowadays, couples know each other better and are alone together much more. Men have traditionally coped with this less well than women, and some continue to make periodic disappearances, literal and emotional.

A deeper change is the modern acceptance of the idea that passionate love can flourish within marriage or within a long-term relationship. Such expectations are in striking contrast to those of the 18th century, when marriage was seen primarily as a financial contract. Weddings were often arranged by the parents, and "love matches" were rare. Much earlier, the court romances of medieval Europe drew a clear distinction between the vows of love and marriage. The 12th-century noblewoman Marie,

Two Lovers Listening to a Cuckoo, by the 18th-century Japanese artist Ippitsusai Buncho, portrays the feeling of wonder we have for everything around us when we are in love.

Comtesse de Champagne, wrote: "Love cannot extend its rights to married persons, for lovers give everything to each other without being forced in any way, as is not the case in marriage."

Romantic love in the 19th century was thought to be compatible with marriage if minds and souls were perfectly attuned. The less cynical modern belief that love can survive marriage, and indeed can grow stronger within it, was encouraged by greater sexual awareness. During the 1960s' "Sexual Revolution", skilled love-making was considered the key to lasting love. Accelerating divorce

From the *Roman de la Rose*, this illustration (below), painted around 1500, depicts a lady and her lover about to enter the garden of love.

This charming bas-relief (left), entitled *A Basket of Loves*, shows the goddess Venus releasing cupids into the world.

Eric Gill's illustration to Chaucer's *Troilus and Cressida* (below) portrays the couple in an embrace. There are no clues in the scene that soon Cressida will be unfaithful.

Introduction

rates have since cast doubt on such a simplistic view, and modern lovers generally believe that knowledge and mutual respect form a stronger foundation for a relationship. This reveals a new approach to love, neither sceptical nor starry-eyed. If a new vision of love is forming, it can only be built on an understanding of the past. The links between sex, love and the changing moods of the human heart remain mysterious. Traditional philosophy, mythology and literature still have much to teach us about love in all its possible manifestations.

THE ANATOMY OF LOVE

Hot beautiful furless animals
Played in a clearing opened by their desire.
THOM GUNN, "ADULTERY"

Thom Gunn's image of lovers as animals playing tells us more about how love came into the world than whole books of intellectual theory. No true anatomy of love can ignore either the primal force of desire or humanity's unique capacity for aesthetic pleasure. It is this capacity that works upon mere instinct and transforms it into something different and marvellous.

Philosophy has always assumed a major role in deciphering the mysteries of love. Some of the most imaginative and influential theories are contained in Plato's *Symposium*, written in the 4th century BCE. His definition of love as "the desire and pursuit of the whole" has often been reinterpreted, but never bettered.

THE GENESIS OF LOVE

Zoologists who have compared the evolution and behaviour of humans and animals think that love began as an advanced form of the pair-bonding also seen in primates. Like us, primates have a long period of dependency on their parents. Such long "childhoods" profoundly influence our emotional ability to form close relationships and to love.

Forces of evolution are also thought by some scientists to play an unconscious

The Bible story of Adam and Eve is shown in this 12th-century Spanish painting. God makes Eve from Adam's rib. Their love is innocent until they taste the forbidden fruit and are banished from the garden of Eden.

role in our selection of a mate. The 19th-century German philosopher Arthur Schopenhauer said that love ensures that we reproduce and is an emotion inseparable from sex. The emotion leads us to search for someone perfectly attuned to our own personality, but remains in essence an individualized sexual impulse, however ethereal.

More recent studies of love as a complex series of chemical reactions have made little progress. Showing that love is chemically different from sexual yearning is beyond the current capabilities of laboratory science. Yet everything tells us that the two states of mind are not the same and that the difference is crucial.

If nature has added an emotion to a physical act, how marvellously humans have developed it! This is perhaps what the French author Honoré de Balzac meant when he wrote: "Love is the poetry of the senses. ... How blasphemous it is to use the word 'love' in connection with the reproduction of the species."

THE MEETING OF SOULS

Swans (above), who mate for life, often appear in myths as bewitched human beings.

In this 18th-century Indian miniature (left), a prince and his lover are shown cocooned in their own world, in flight from reality.

"I cannot live without my soul," cries lost Heathcliff in *Wuthering Heights*, inconsolable after the death of his beloved Catherine Earnshaw. Behind Emily Brontë's novel about two kindred spirits who are haunted and tormented by separation lies a long tradition of Western and Eastern mysticism in which love is centred in the soul.

Plato's *Symposium*, which was written in the 4th century BCE, first described love as a longing for union with an unconscious, ideal image. In this conception of love, Eros embodies a purely spiritual desire. Response to the external beauty of an individual body is caused by the soul's natural affinity with perfection rather than by any sexual impulse.

The Platonic concept of soul love

The Meeting of Souls

has influenced ideas in both Christian and Muslim societies for centuries. To the medieval mind, the theory perfectly explained why mere sexual fulfilment still left the heart yearning and the soul unfulfilled. Themes of spiritual union dominated Islamic love poetry. This so-called "higher" form of love was also celebrated by the great poets of the Italian Renaissance, Dante and Petrarch. The latter described Laura, his inspiration, in terms of religious adoration: she was "the source of that uplifting grace which guides us by the proper path to Heaven".

The notion of souls loving for all eternity was revived as a literary theme in the 19th century and since then it has never entirely disappeared. In its most extreme form, the elevation of the soul above the body led to the ideal of lovers preferring a joint death to the consummation of their passion. The more humanist perspective is that perfect love integrates body and soul.

THE LONGING FOR UNION

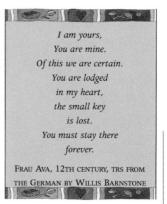

In nearly all creation myths, the primal state involves a single, total principle. This may be a god, a cosmic ocean, pure Self or the force of chaos, but the original being in each case must divide itself to produce the diversity of living things. For centuries, sexual desire and longing were believed to arise from the separation of an originally bisexual or androgynous entity. For example, in Indian myth the creator god Brahma forces the divine Shiva, half-male, half-female, to expel his female side, Parvati. She slips back into him after replicating herself as a female deity, and Shiva falls in love with the Parvati double.

Such stories contain an essential truth about love: it is in part a longing to escape our sense of insufficiency.

> *I am yours,*
> *You are mine.*
> *Of this we are certain.*
> *You are lodged*
> *in my heart,*
> *the small key*
> *is lost.*
> *You must stay there*
> *forever.*
>
> FRAU AVA, 12TH CENTURY, TRS FROM
> THE GERMAN BY WILLIS BARNSTONE

The Longing for Union

EROTIC LOVE

The link between sex and love is so powerful that the word "erotic" has become synonymous with the arousal of sexual desire. In our own times, Eros appears to be restricted to physical passion, balanced on a knife-edge between desire and fulfilment. For, as the literature of unhappy love reveals, sexual fulfilment can paradoxically extinguish desire. The greatest intensity of erotic love may therefore occur in the moment before desire achieves its object.

A painted miniature (below) depicts the Hindu god Krishna and his love Radha.

The belief that Eros – in the sense of pure physical desire – consists of a longing for something beyond reach¹ is evoked in John Keats' famous "Ode on a Grecian Urn": "More happy love! more happy, happy love! / Forever warm and

Gustav Klimt's painting *Danaë* (right) shows the princess of Argos being visited by Zeus in the form of a shower of gold.

Erotic Love

still to be enjoyed, / Forever panting, and forever young." The happy love is embodied by a maiden, placed just beyond her lover's grasp in a scene painted on the urn. This instant before union is firmly fixed in time and therefore protected from the changing seasons of love experienced in the real world.

The paradox that desire can disappear when physically satisfied has preoccupied writers from many diverse cultures. Plato's solution was to see the consummation of sexual passion as a stage on the way to a higher goal, allowing love itself to persist as a sense of unassuaged longing.

The ebb and flow of desire can possess an emotional as well as a physical aspect. The French writer Simone Weil has described the tortuous fluctuations of human love: "I want the person I love to love me. However, if he is totally devoted to me he does not exist any longer and I cease to love him. And as long as he is not totally devoted to me, he does not love me enough."

This ancient Greek red-figure cup is decorated with the lovers Ariadne and Dionysus, accompanied by the god Eros. The story of Ariadne, who was abandoned and rescued before finding happiness, shows the complexities and dangers of erotic love.

The Private Pleasure of Emperor Jahangir features a pair of lovers in a garden setting. Virility and sexual prowess were often considered positive attributes in a ruler.

Erotic Love

Erotic love is essentially a maelstrom of conflicting impulses and sensations. Sex is an integral part, of course, but cannot be considered its ultimate object. If this were so, people who continue to make each other happy sexually would have no reason to fall out of love – but there is plenty of evidence that they often do. Pure lust, although sometimes confused with the infatuation stage of love, is a much less challenging emotion. It is quite possible to have a great loveless sex affair. Indeed, the Roman philosopher and poet Lucretius pointed out in the 1st century BCE that love may actually distract from sensual pleasure. The bittersweet complexity of erotic love stems from the fact that it is precariously focused on a single person and calls into play an infinite number of wishes, needs and obscure desires, all charged with the high explosive of sex.

THE PSYCHOLOGY OF LOVE

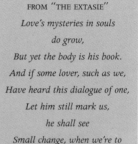

FROM *"THE EXTASIE"*

Love's mysteries in souls
do grow,
But yet the body is his book.
And if some lover, such as we,
Have heard this dialogue of one,
Let him still mark us,
he shall see
Small change, when we're to
bodies gone.

JOHN DONNE (1572–1631)

Love is the most poetic emotion that we know, and at the same time one of our most basic needs. Its associated experiences and fantasies are delineated in the myths and fairytales of innumerable societies and cultures, yet its causes and impact still escape our full comprehension. It has been mocked as a transient illusion and celebrated as a blind, biological imperative – the expression of an immensely powerful life force.

The idea of love as a biological drive provided a starting point for the revolutionary theories of Sigmund Freud. His psychology of love was grounded in the belief that the role of the *libido*, operating at the unconscious level of animal instinct, had been vastly underestimated in identifying both the source of love

The biblical story of the temptation of Adam and Eve has long been used to condemn female desire. The serpent is often depicted with a woman's head and torso.

In this detail of *The World Before the Flood* by Hieronymus Bosch (ca. 1505), the world is full of strange lusts and pleasures.

Emma Turpin's *Mother and her Children* (above) represents conflicting impulses within a woman.

(Left) In Greek myth, Milanion throws golden apples in front of Atalanta to beat her in a race and win her hand.

and the seemingly mysterious process by which we select a love object.

Freud was the first to propose a coherent theory of love based on scientific principles. He concluded that we fall in love because we follow rules buried below the level of our conscious thought. Psychoanalysis seemed to reveal that these rules were derived from our infancy and in particular from our sensual attachment to those who loved us – or those who

The Psychology of Love

did not love us, although we longed for them to do so. Freud's theories have been much criticized, yet he remains the 20th century's most influential psychologist.

The interdependence of male and female needs, also emphasized by Freud, was first perceived many centuries earlier. In Chinese philosophy, the whole universe is infused with the opposing yet complementary powers of *yin* and *yang*, representing essential female and male qualities. The symbol for *yin* and *yang* epitomizes their mutual dependence – two perfectly integrated halves unite to form a complete, harmonious circle.

Many modern psychologists believe that our psychosexual identity contains male and female aspects, and that they play some part in determining with whom we fall in love. The importance of the first

This illustration comes from a manual of social etiquette for women, written in the 15th century by Christine de Pisan.

few years of life is also now thought to be considerable. In relationships as adults we tend to seek a replacement for the love and attention once experienced in childhood – perhaps accounting for the almost magical, absolute certainty with which lovers frequently seem to recognize one another.

Falling in love involves an often contradictory mixture of sexual desire, emotions and values. The paradoxes of love swiftly become apparent: a longing for closeness contends with the need to assert our own identity, and erotic desire itself is episodic. The need to feel a sense of power in a relationship – and yet also have the confidence to surrender control – fluctuates from day to day. Our ability to balance these diverse psychosexual demands determines the success or otherwise of our love relationships.

For most people, despite – or even because of – its many contradictions and difficulties, love is still an emotion to be valued above all else.

The Psychology of Love

Since we through war awhile must part
Sweetheart, and learn to lose
Daily use
Of all that satisfied our heart:
Lay up those secrets and those powers
Wherewith you pleased and cherished me
these two years:

Now we must draw, as plants would,
On tubers stored in a better season,
Our honey and heaven;
Only our love can store such food.
Is this to make a god of absence?
A new-born monster to steal our sustenance?

We cannot quite cast out lack and pain.
Let him remain – what he may devour
We can well spare:
He never can tap this, the true vein.
I have no words to tell you what you were,
But when you are sad, think, Heaven could
give no more.

ANNE RIDLER, "At Parting"

*There is a strong wall about
  me to protect me:
It is built of the words you
  have said to me.*

*There are swords about me to
  keep me safe:
They are the kisses of your lips.*

*Before me goes a shield to
  guard me from harm:
It is the shadow of your arms
  between me and danger.*

*All the wishes of my mind
  know your name,
And the white desires of
  my heart
They are acquainted with you.
The cry of my body for
  completeness,
That is a cry to you.
My blood beats out your name
  to me, unceasing, pitiless
Your name, your name.*

MARY CAROLYN DAVIES,
"Love Song"

Love and Beauty

LOVE AND BEAUTY

This miniature shows Krishna about to shoot Radha with the arrow of desire.

The swiftest cue for love has always been human beauty, striking with the speed and force of an arrow. The relationship between love and perceived beauty has been celebrated in widely different cultures for centuries. Islamic love poetry is devoted almost exclusively to the praise of ideal beauty. In the ancient Greek pantheon, Aphrodite is the goddess of beauty as well as love.

As a motive for love, beauty is much less popular with rationalists. Voltaire, for example, ridiculed it in his play *Candide*: the hero's passionate love for the beautiful Cunégonde is thwarted for so long that when he finally marries her she has become bad-tempered and hideous.

Beauty is a dangerous gift, both for the beautiful and for those who love them. Beautiful people often feel that they are not loved for themselves and that because of this they will be deserted as their beauty fades. They may also be narcissistic or egotistical – though by no means always. Our ideas of beauty are peculiarly subjective, responding to expressive qualities of personality and character as well as contemporary fashion

Raphael's painting of the Three Graces, the handmaidens of Aphrodite.

Love and Beauty

Like female beauty, male beauty is a powerful catalyst for romantic love. Hippolyte Flandrin's *Young Man on a Rock* (ca. 1830) portrays a youth, apparently unaware of his charms.

and taste. A lover's capacity to idealize the Beloved can paradoxically accompany a clear perception of their physical faults. Perfect beauty may sometimes appear an inscrutable mask; blemishes may be precisely what touch the heart of someone in love. Once we are experiencing love for a real person, an abstract physical ideal becomes much less relevant. Beauty certainly inspires love, but cannot alone keep it.

LOVE AND VIRTUE

Erotic love and moral virtue have not always been seen as natural bedfellows. In the Islamic faith, as well as in many pagan traditions, secular love was seen as an ennobling emotion, able to inspire artistic creativity, courage and devotion. However, in the early Christian Church the only pure love was considered to be the love of God. In the 12th century, the "Song of Songs", the Bible's sole poem celebrating the sweetness of erotic love, was even interpreted as an allegory of the Virgin Mary.

The religious reformer Martin Luther acknowledged the force of sexual desire

This Chantilly enamel box of the 18th century (above) is decorated with a sedate couple in bed. The union of marriage was seen as a source of civic virtue as well as of personal happiness and wellbeing.

Love and Virtue

This 16th-century portrait (left) uses the symbols of a gold chain and lemons to reflect the belief that a good and honourable marriage would be wealthy and fruitful.

and rejected the idea that marriage was inferior to chastity. Yet for centuries, Protestant and Catholic doctrine taught that physical passion should be kept strictly within the bounds of social duty.

The distance between love and virtue narrowed dramatically in the 19th

Throughout the ages, jewelry has been given and worn by lovers as a pledge of commitment. This cameo of a royal couple (above) dates from the 3rd century BCE.

In former times, the fiery, desirable woman in this painting by Emma Turpin (left) might have been seen as a seductress. However, to modern eyes she represents a benevolent, protective force.

Love and Virtue

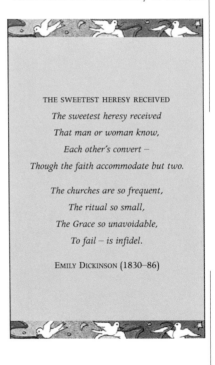

THE SWEETEST HERESY RECEIVED

The sweetest heresy received
That man or woman know,
Each other's convert –
Though the faith accommodate but two.

The churches are so frequent,
The ritual so small,
The Grace so unavoidable,
To fail – is infidel.

EMILY DICKINSON (1830–86)

Love and Divine

century. Marrying for love began to be widely accepted, and poets such as the atheistic Shelley wrote of love as a heightening of moral sensibility. The philosopher John Stuart Mill believed that an ideal marriage should involve an ethical education of like-minded individuals: "each can enjoy the luxury of looking up to the other ... " By the end of the 19th century, love in marriage had been virtually deified. Even for people who were not deeply religious, marriage was seen as a solemn and binding commitment.

The great change that has occurred since the early 20th century is that physical passion no longer needs the sanctity of marriage to be virtuous – it is now considered to be one aspect of a shared ideal. Whether modern love lasts or not is less a matter of law or religion than of continuing mutual love and respect – which now depends, perhaps more than ever before, on the personal virtue of each partner.

LOVE AND FRIENDSHIP

Lovers Walking, painted by Pellizza Da Volpede, captures the intimate moments of friendship in love.

The time-honoured protestation that someone is not a lover but "just a good friend" seems to reveal a vast gulf between the two conditions. However, as many of us proceed to discover, this mutable and ambivalent boundary may be both possible and pleasurable to cross. The "marriage of true minds", celebrated by Shakespeare in one of his great love sonnets, lies at the core of our deepest friendships, and has often been perceived as one of the noblest causes of love. Mental affinity may not capture the heart as swiftly as beauty, but it can nevertheless provide the basis for deep love – and passion can develop from it.

The delicate balance between the emotional commitment of friendship and acknowledgment of love has been a source of fascination for centuries. Sigmund Freud believed that latent

Love and Friendship

Love and Friendship

Picnic in May, a 19th-century painting by Szinyei Merse Pal, depicts the elements of flirtation that are present in most deep friendships between men and women.

Love and Friendship

sexual impulses always underlie intense friendship. Yet other cultures, both ancient and modern, have praised friendship as the purest, least selfish form of love.

Non-sexual friendship between men and men, women and women or men and women can create emotional bonds as strong as all but the most intense forms of erotic love – and often more enduring. Byron, who described erotic love as "a sort of hostile transaction", believed that men and women made excellent friends if they were not lovers. Yet a really happy physical relationship tells us that friendship and sensuality can be combined – and must be if it is to last. A true friendship, according to 19th-century Romantics, is a deep spiritual and emotional affinity: a tie of mutual sym-pathy, without which neither friendship nor love will endure.

ILLUSION AND REALITY

"Love is the son of deceit and father of illusion," wrote the Spanish scholar Miguel de Unamuno in *The Tragic Sense of Life* (1913). Such an anguished disbelief in the reality of love is probably shared by anyone who has suddenly and inexplicably stopped loving another, or has been betrayed by someone they thought cared for them.

The sometimes ephemeral nature of erotic love may indeed enable cynics to dismiss the whole emotion as an illusion. If real, how can it possibly disappear in the blink of an eye? Infatuations that depend purely on physical chemistry are particularly prone to sudden evaporation. If physical desire wanes, or if other values begin to influence the relationship, coldness or dislike can follow with disconcerting speed.

In Hinduism even lasting love is regarded as one aspect of *maya*, or illusion. The world – and everything in

it – was formed from the creative power of *maya*, and so human love, in some ways our deepest, most vain attachment to the world of the senses, is always tinged with an awareness of its ephemeral nature. Nevertheless, love is as "real" as any other human construct. Love is not only an emotion, but also a

human quality, as impossible to deny as, for example, truthfulness or courage. The consequences of love may well be short-lived or unpredictable, but they are also dramatic, visible and real.

We may often fall in love under the spell of a self-created vision. In Flaubert's novel, Emma Bovary's fascination with

The story of Cupid and Psyche (above; page 71) reveals how, despite the fascination of a dream lover, we eventually need to know his or her true identity.

Illusion and Reality

The mirror is a symbol of love and beauty. Robert Anning Bell's *Cupid's Mirror* shows how the images we have of ourselves and the world around can be transformed when we fall in love.

the idle philanderer Rodolphe is no less intense for having been founded on fantasy: "a phantom composed of her most passionate memories, her most enjoyable books, and her strongest desires." Sharpened by imagination, her love soon disintegrates in, the cold light of experience. Fantasies of love in the real world are often similarly inclined to evaporate if analyzed.

The initial stages of a love affair may be sustained largely through illusion. Love is far more than "falling in love", however. It is also a stripping away of illusion to acknowledge and cherish the fallible human within. It is this kind of clear-sighted love that provides, for many people, the most "real" and enduring experience in life.

LOVE AND LONELINESS

On the Tiles, a woodcut by Eric Gill, illustrates our instinct to curl up and hide when we feel isolated.

The human need to escape from solitude is intimately linked with love. We often seek love affairs to avoid loneliness, yet the greatest isolation of all may be encountered in the final, faltering stages of a relationship. The special intensity of first love may in part be a response to the sudden miracle of sensual intimacy. So overwhelming is this that parting from each other even for an hour, let alone for a period of days, becomes virtually unbearable. It is as if part of ourself is being dragged away from us. In an established relationship, being apart is never quite the same as the feeling of loneliness, as we continue to feel the presence of the beloved in an almost

Love and Loneliness

physical way. If a lover is lost permanently, the sense of renewed loneliness can be devastating.

Consciously or not, our human need to escape loneliness is always a part of loving someone – which is not to say that love removes the need. Those who love the most intensely are often the loneliest, suffering most from absences, misunderstandings, betrayals, or the eventual loss of love. This is another of love's bittersweet paradoxes. We often feel that we would die without the beloved. Yet in order to achieve a successful, lasting relationship, we must also learn how to survive alone.

Love and Loneliness

This painting by Emma Turpin shows a woman alone, gathering fruit and flowers from a largely barren landscape.

Tonight I can write the saddest lines.

Write, for example, 'The night is shattered
and the blue stars shiver in the distance.'

The night wind revolves in the sky and sings.

Tonight, I can write the saddest lines.
I loved her, and sometimes she loved me too.

Through nights like this one, I held her in my arms.
I kissed her again and again under the endless sky.

She loved me, sometimes I loved her too.
How could one not have loved her great still eyes.

Tonight I can write the saddest lines.
To think that I do not have her. To feel that I have
 lost her.

To hear the immense night, still more immense
 without her.
And the verse falls to the soul like dew to the pasture.

What does it matter that my love could not keep her.
The night is shattered and she is not with me.

This is all. In the distance someone is singing. In
 the distance.
My soul is not satisfied that it has lost her.

PABLO NERUDA *(1904–73)*, "The Saddest Lines",
trs from the Spanish by W. S. Merwin

First time he kissed me, he but only
  kissed
The fingers of this hand wherewith I write,
And ever since it grew more clean and
  white, ..
Slow to world-greetings ... quick with its
  "Oh, list,"
When the angels speak. A ring of amethyst
I could not wear here plainer to my sight,
Than that first kiss. The second passed
  in height
The first, and sought the forehead, and
  half missed,
Half falling on the hair. O beyond meed!
That was the chrism of love, which love's
  own crown,
With sanctifying sweetness, did precede.
The third, upon my lips, was folded down
In perfect, purple state! since when, indeed,
I have been proud and said, "My Love,
  my own."

ELIZABETH BARRETT BROWNING *(1806–61),*
"Sonnet from the Portuguese XXXVIII"

DIMENSIONS OF THE HEART

I am two fooles, I know
For loving, and for saying so
In whining Poetry;
But where's that wiseman, that would not be I,
If she would not deny?
JOHN DONNE (1573–1631), "THE TRIPLE FOOLE"

Writers may argue about the origin of love, but none disputes the bewildering range of its emotional scale. Being in love may produce our greatest happiness, but also sometimes our deepest pain.

Love has several different ages, from the serenity of enduring commitment to the overwhelming beauty of youthful love, when the sensory world pours in upon us and changes everything. The search for lasting love is always uncertain: passion may be unrequited, or betrayed, or simply eroded by time, yet in its tumultuous impact, love reveals the most surprising dimensions of the human heart.

SYMPTOMS OF LOVE

Symptoms of Love

This Persian manuscript shows two lovers totally absorbed in each other.

So remarkable are the symptoms of lovesickness that they were considered in medieval Europe to be a physical or mental malady to which the noble-born (by implication, the more sensitive) were particularly prone. Classic symptoms of the yearning lover included sleeplessness, nightmares, hallucinations, pallor, lack of concentration and loss of appetite. A manic elation might be succeeded by extreme misery and a hopeless feeling that the adored one was a paragon of beauty and virtue far beyond reach. These effects were compounded by sensations of breathlessness and a pounding heart. A languid demeanour and piteous sighs became a form of medieval courtship which any self-respecting lover felt obliged to display.

Lovers, of course, have always believed that their sickness can only be cured by the responsive presence of the beloved.

However, through history a range of remedies has been proposed, from the pragmatic to the absurd. In the 11th century Constantine's *Viaticum* claimed that Eros was a disease of men's brains, and recommended recourse to prostitutes as a means of calming the inflammation. Priests advised less radical cures, such as travel, games and regular bathing. Magnetism, microbes and astronomical influences were suspected causes of lovesickness in the 17th century, and as late as 1904, Dr Charles Féré compared the impact of love at first sight to an electric shock or spasm.

Modern research does reveal a correlation between high levels of

THE SONG OF SONGS 2:3–5
As the apple tree among the trees
of the wood,
so is my beloved among the sons.
I sat down under his shadow with
great delight,
and his fruit was sweet to my taste.
He brought me to the banqueting house,
and his banner over me was love.
Stay me with flagons,
comfort me with apples:
for I am sick of love.

KING JAMES BIBLE, 1611

Symptoms of Love

neurotransmitters and the mood swings of lovesick romantics. Injections of adrenaline can induce similar symptoms of physical arousal – a pounding heart, trembling knees and hands, flushing and sweating – revealing that emotions are simply different interpretations of psychological stress. Self-delusion also plays a considerable role in our experience of love's symptoms. Attraction to another may be hastily dismissed by the person who feels it as "mere" infatuation. The impulse of love is closely linked with that of sexual desire, and only after disentangling the confusion can we decide whether we are "in love" or not.

Even if we recognize the symptoms of love, our immediate reaction is unpredictable. In the presence of someone for whom we feel an instant physical attraction, we may feel tongue-tied and excruciatingly shy. More sophisticated lovers, however, respond to such an encounter by displaying a sudden and dazzling amount of poise and wit.

FIRST LOVE

For all the strong, complex passions that it arouses, love has a childlike side. In acquiring sexual experience, there is always some nostalgia for the loss of innocence, some longing for love to continue as a pure and delicate spirit.

Parents often project this longing on to their adolescent children, wishing young lovers to remain suspended in a kind of ethereal bliss. The perfect archetype of this yearning is the story of Cupid and Psyche, told by the Roman writer, Apuleius, in the 2nd century CE. Having aroused the jealousy of the goddess Venus by her great beauty, Psyche is visited nightly by a gentle, sweet-smelling bridegroom whose identity she is forbidden to know. Her evil sisters persuade Psyche to spy upon

This Renaissance painting, which is attributed to G.B. Bertucci, depicts Daphnis and Chloë, two foundlings brought up by shepherds, who gradually fall in love.

her lover while he is asleep. Her lamp reveals the beautiful form of the winged god Cupid, one of whose arrows pricks her as she plays with it, drawing blood. He wakes and flees when oil from the lamp falls on his shoulder. Yet the story ends happily: after completing a series of dangerous trials, Psyche is rescued by Cupid from a death-like trance. Although born mortal, Psyche is permitted to join the gods and marry her lover.

Cupid and Psyche seem to represent an almost unisexual couple – a romantic vision of young lovers who in their graceful and delicate sensuality are almost mirror images of one another.

The American scholar Jean Hagstrum has suggested that the idea of delicate love may anticipate "an influential modern idea that to feminize life may in fact be to civilize it". The story of Cupid and Psyche may perhaps be interpreted as an allegory of young lovers discovering that they are not frighteningly different from each other.

In *Amity*, a painting by Bernard Fleetwood Walker, the friendship of two young adolescents is gently tinted by their burgeoning sexuality.

First Love

LOVE'S HESITATIONS

Love is a struggle between our longing to fuse ourselves with another and our fear that in the process we may lose our own identity and freedom. If we do not understand the nature of this conflict, we may interpret normal feelings of hesitation as evidence that we are not really in love. Oddly enough, hesitation can often mean the opposite – that we are passing from a phase of infatuation and idealization to one in which we may begin to love a real person.

This transition is hard for narcissistic people – those who have transferred their self-love to an ideal Other and resent any faults or weaknesses in the image they have created. The heavy

This Elizabethan miniature (left) by Nicholas Hilliard shows a tormented young man in a rose garden.

demands that we make on the .person we want to love are among the greatest obstacles to making a lasting commitment. The strong and the proud may also feel they are showing weakness by admitting that they need someone.

Shows of indifference, hesitation, reluctance or outright hostility are, of course, also part of the age-old game of love. Women were once expected to

Love's Hesitations

Understanding our own hesitations may be hard, but realizing that the one we love also has doubts can be devastating. In Emma Turpin's painting (right) a wary lover is approaching a seemingly uninterested woman. The scene is overlooked by a distant, Cupid-like figure.

75

pretend to spurn men's advances – and were valued all the more if they did.

However, feelings of ambivalence are more than just a ruse. Most of us feel

In Nelly Erichsen's *The Orchard* a lover tries to overcome his hesitant sweetheart's uncertainties.

alternating desire and resistance, and even alternating love and hate. The Irish poet Thomas Moore wrote: "When I loved you, I can't but allow / I had many an exquisite minute / But the scorn that I feel for you now / Hath even more luxury in it!" Hatred can, in fact, sometimes be a deep-rooted psychological defence against making the ultimate commitment of loving someone.

THE BUNGLER

You glow in my heart
Like the flames of uncounted candles.
But when I go to warm my hands,
My clumsiness overturns the light,
And then I stumble
Against the tables and chairs.

AMY LOWELL (1874–1925)

Love's Hesitations

NEED AND PROTECTION

Need and Protection

"My love is selfish. I cannot breathe without you," Keats wrote to Fanny Brawne. It would seem that need is part of all human love.

Protective love – parental love, for example – is a form of unconditional love which is seldom present in adult relationships. However, lovers may assume parent-child roles, one partner predominantly protecting and giving, the other constantly needing and receiving love.

Before our own time, the idea that men were protectors and women were in need of protection was one of the most deeply ingrained of all cultural traditions. Modern writings on love are very aware of the dynamics of power in a relationship: the relative strength of each partner is fluid, dependent upon individuals and changing circumstances, and not determined solely by gender.

Need-love can be stifling if it turns into an addiction. Some lovers become so emotionally demanding that they are impossible to satisfy. In the best kind of love, both partners need and protect, give and receive – and admit to doing so.

Need and Protection

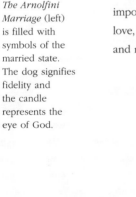

Jan van Eyck's *The Arnolfini Marriage* (left) is filled with symbols of the married state. The dog signifies fidelity and the candle represents the eye of God.

UNREQUITED LOVE

The more powerfully we are attracted to someone we meet, the harder it is to believe that the electricity that we feel crackling between us may not be a reciprocal current, but simply the reflected energy of our own emotion. To discover this later on in a relationship can be even more confusing.

If it is any comfort, this painful realization is one that nearly everyone makes at some time in their lives. According to Ovid's myth of the beautiful youth Adonis, the goddess of love herself was humiliated when Adonis impatiently rejected her advances. In Shakespeare's poem "Venus and Adonis", Cupid's arrow is powerless to affect Adonis. Venus, bewildered and frustrated, accuses him of an obsessive self-love: "Narcissus so himself foresook / And died to kiss his shadow in the brook."

Psychologists tell us that narcissism is indeed one of the reasons why some people are unable to respond to love. They may wish to be treated as their ideal self. Or they may have formulated an imaginary, idealized Other, so specific that the chance of such a threatening encounter is fairly remote. However, this is an extreme case. We are much more likely to suffer unrequited love simply because we have made the mistake of assuming that our own feelings are experienced by another. There is really no reason to expect another person to reciprocate our love – unless we overlook the fact that passion is not a rational or logical experience. Love can strike us with such force that we tend to forget how singular it is. It may distort our perception, allowing

In this 15th-century tapestry, a courtly lover surrenders his heart to his lady, seated in a sensual garden of love.

Unrequited Love

us to make fools of ourselves as a result. A famous example is the sour steward Malvolio in Shakespeare's *Twelfth Night*, who absurdly believes himself to be loved by the lady whom he serves. Yet he has nothing on which to base this supposition but a cryptic letter, designed to tease him.

Unrequited Love

Some people deliberately choose to love someone inaccessible because it avoids all possibility of being rejected or disappointed. A truer – and more agonizing – form of unrequited love involves a refusal to accept rejection. The emotional charge is sustained by a desperate hope that this love will one day be returned, together with an inconsolable longing. The Greeks named this longing after a special god, Antieros, brother of Eros. It can be a creative impetus and has produced some of the world's most poignant poetry – notably the many love poems W. B. Yeats wrote to the Irish beauty Maude Gonne, who was to marry another man.

LOVE AND JEALOUSY

One of the greatest challenges in love is to contend with the range of darker emotions it may unleash in us. Jealousy, or "love's shadow", is one of the most frequently encountered, a feeling which we almost universally disdain but which is integral to our experience of passion.

Love and Jealousy

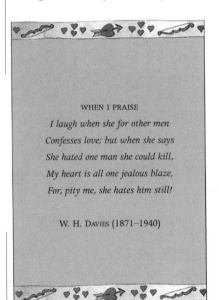

WHEN I PRAISE

I laugh when she for other men
Confesses love; but when she says
She hated one man she could kill,
My heart is all one jealous blaze,
For, pity me, she hates him still!

W. H. DAVIES (1871–1940)

This painting by Ingres depicts an encounter of the lovers Francesca da Rimini and Paolo, her husband's brother. The adulterous couple were executed by her husband in 1389.

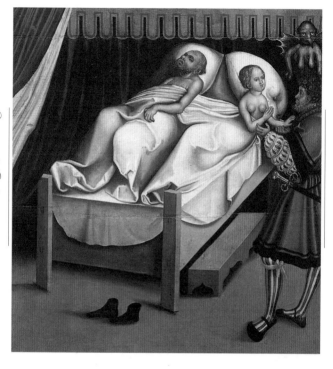

Love and Jealousy

 .   Intense jealousy is often also the first sign that we are in love. If we have missed or undervalued all the other signals, the appearance of a rival tends to concentrate the mind wonderfully.

In Cranach's painting from the early 16th century, a beautiful woman slips out of bed into the arms of her lover. Her husband continues to sleep, while a medieval devil views the scene with approval.

Psychologists have identified three types of jealousy – delusional, projected and competitive. Delusional jealousy, peculiarly dangerous and cruelly unfair, is the form dramatized in Shakespeare's *Othello*, where the villainous Iago plants and nourishes Othello's insecurity.

Projected jealousy is less malignant, but it may also destroy love if we let it. This type of jealousy perceives harmless flirtations or friendships to be disloyalties in themselves. Such unfounded fears can drive us to attempt to restrict the other's freedom or even to spy on him or her.

Competitive jealousy, by contrast, is often completely justified, for a real betrayal is one of the most acutely painful experiences in love. Less easy to negotiate is the antagonism provoked by straightforward rivalry for another's love. A common form of retaliation is the teasing attempt to inspire reciprocal jealousy in the beloved. This is often a successful tactic, as long as the game-playing does not become out of control.

Love and Jealousy

LOVE TRIANGLES

Love Triangles

One of the most frequent reasons for lack of happiness in love is the existence of a triangle of some sort. A rival is often involved at either the beginning or the end of a relationship, leading to a three-way situation in which at least one person feels anguished – and sometimes all three.

A fundamental tenet of traditional romantic love is that it is fixed upon a single other soul. Yet a great deal of romantic literature is dominated by triangular relationships. Courtly love, because it was mainly adulterous, itself involved a triangle, as in the story of the legendary King

The Merciless Lady, a painting by the Pre-Raphaelite artist Dante Gabriel Rossetti, shows a girl looking on helplessly as her lover becomes fascinated by another woman.

Arthur, his queen Guinevere and her lover, Arthur's trusted friend Sir Lancelot.

Yet some who find themselves in a triangle discover that their experience of love is sharpened and even enhanced by it. The exquisite pain of being unsure that they are loved completely is, for certain lovers, the essence of passion. They may need the spur of jealousy to believe fully that they are in love. For others, deliberately maintaining a love triangle offers a dangerous sense of excitement – and perhaps an unacknowledged sense of emotional security. Such a situation enables lovers to avoid the risks inherent in making any final commitment to a singular love – which may threaten their valued personal freedom. Instead, the impermanence creates its own security, and they are able to maintain two lovers in a tantalizing state of indecision – at least for a while.

Love Triangles

Duels offered a traditional way for gentlemen to dispose of their rivals in love. The custom was only outlawed in the 19th century.

Drink to me only with thine eyes,
And I will pledge with mine;
Or leave a kiss but in the cup,
And I'll not look for wine.
The thirst that from the soul doth rise,
Doth ask a drink divine:
But might I of Jove's nectar sup,
I would not change for thine.

I sent thee late a rosy wreath,
Not so much honouring thee,
As giving it a hope, that there
It could not withered be.
But thou thereon did'st only breathe,
And sent'st it back to me;
Since when it grows and smells, I swear,
Not of itself, but thee.

BEN JONSON *(1572–1637)*, "Song: To Celia"

When I lie prone above your lovely face
Your eyes reveal strange glints of white, of black,
And my whole bloodstream seethes along its track
Right to the heart itself the colours race.
What they disclose is Love, who changes place,
Now low, now high, bow bent and staring back.
Shot after shot I suffer his attack.
Reason, if I'm deluded, state your case!

Such loss of self-control these visions bring
I would betray my father and my king,
My sisters, brothers, mother – yes, and France.
So crazed I am, having drunk long and well
A venom spurted by our dalliance
Out of the eyes which hold me in their spell.

PIERRE DE RONSARD *(1524–85)*, "Meslanges,
2, VI", *trs from the French by Laurence Kitchin*

LOVE AND MADNESS

"To live and to suffer – heaven, hell – that is what I want to feel," wrote Julie de Lespinasse, mistress of the 18th-century French philosopher and mathematician Jean d'Alembert. Her ardent love letters to him expressed the desire, which is shared by many romantic lovers, to "love as one must love: excessively, to the point of madness and despair".

The concept of love as an all-consuming passion, a terrible obsession sweeping away reason or conventions, was a grand theme of many 19th-century romantic novels and operas. However, it has a much older history than that. The extremes of human love have always been seen as a divine

In an illustration from *The Book of Good Morals*, two characters' alter egos try to persuade them to act irrationally.

There is an undercurrent of violence in this late 18th-century painting of two lovers.

Love and Madness

madness. Countless portraits of women as sphinx-like creatures concealing smouldering passions betray men's fears of arousing a venomous or insatiable lover. From classical literature to Hollywood movies, a series of vengeful harpies embody the male fear that love may, literally, drive women crazy.

In reality, it may frequently be the sanest, most rational thinkers of both sexes who become unhinged by an obsessive love, often for a wildly unsuitable object. The English essayist William Hazlitt, for example, recorded his entirely absurd, passionate feelings of jealousy over his landlady's daughter, only half his own age.

Psychologists describe this type of love as a form of utter selfishness. Elevated to the status of a god, love demands an obedience so complete that we become deaf to our own conscience. Mad, passionate love excuses much, but we are still troubled if it is used to justify abandoning everything else.

LOVE AND LAUGHTER

The bacchanalian fever that swept through Europe at the end of the 19th century led to many extraordinary romances.

Cruel though laughter can seem to a lover whose heart is breaking, humour is an essential ingredient in successful relationships – sometimes the key one. If it can be endured, self-mockery is an invaluable corrective to the miseries of obsessive love.

The old Arabic concept of love as a serious art form, with its elaborate rituals, may itself have been paradoxically based on humour. The historian Theodore Zeldin has suggested that the surprising Bedouin tolerance of joking familiarities between women and visiting strangers first helped to break down restrictive

Love and Laughter

Love and Laughter

This 18th-century needlework panel, entitled *Spring*, celebrates the carefree joys of youthful love.

convention. This in turn facilitated many later adventures of passionate love. "Of love, the first part is jesting and the last part right earnestness," wrote the influential Moorish theologian Ibn Hazm in the 11th century.

Erotic love, especially if it involves breaking rules and the consequent risks of exposure, is always poised on the edge of farce. The master of love and comedy is Shakespeare, for whom courtship is essentially a matter of wit and mirth. Even the youthful, tragic and idealistic Juliet is able to laugh at herself. Humour is seen as one of the greatest female weapons of courtship: among Shakespeare's most attractive and verbally agile heroines are Beatrice in *Much Ado About Nothing* and Viola in *Twelfth Night*. In *As You Like It*, the charming Rosalind skilfully trades jests with the court fool, and warns her own love, Orlando: "Make the doors fast upon a woman's wit, and it will out at the casement; shut that and 'twill out at the key-hole; stop that, 'twill fly with the smoke out at the chimney."

Comedy has always been love's safety valve. Teasing is an essential way in which we test the strength of a new relationship as well as a way of holding someone at arms' length until we are more confident that we know what our feelings for one another are. Few things are as binding as shared laughter, nor is there anything so divisive as finding that the person we think we love has a different sense of humour – or worse still, none at all. Humour has to be part of any lasting relationship, if only as a device to end quarrels in which both have taken up positions that can only be defused by a shared joke.

At masked balls, guests' inhibitions were often released by their facial disguises. The events offered a tantalizing juxtaposition of secret intimacy within a very public sphere.

Love and Laughter

LASTING LOVE

Lasting Love

This Greek funeral relief (above) depicts a married couple who hoped to remain united after death.

"Happily ever after" is usually where the story ends in all the fairytales of love. Lasting love is not the stuff of romantic fiction because the edge of pursuit, drama, danger, uncertainty and, we assume, wild physical passion, has gone. Readers prefer stories of unhappy love. Paradoxically, lasting love sounds almost dull by comparison – yet it is what most lovers seek.

Perhaps tradition has implanted in our hearts the idea that love is ephemeral. In medieval stories of courtly love, most romances ended on a tragic note. It was thought that if every obstacle to love were removed and the lovers married, their passion would soon dwindle and disappear. The belief that marriage is compatible with romantic love is a recent and predominantly Western one.

A few great writers have always stood out

MEN SAY THE PASSIONS SHOULD GROW OLD

Men say the passions should grow old
With passing years; my heart
Is incorruptible as gold,
'Tis my immortal part.
Nor is there any god can lay
On love the finger of decay.

"MICHAEL FIELD", THE PEN NAME OF
KATHERINE BRADLEY (1846–1914) AND
EDITH COOPER (1862–1914)

Vincent van Gogh's *The Siesta* (left) portrays a couple resting quietly together after a hard morning's labour.

Lasting Love

against the prevailing cynicism. One of Shakespeare's greatest sonnets celebrates a deeper conception of love: "Love's not Time's fool, though rosy lips and cheeks / Within his bending sickle's compass come / Love alters not with his brief hours and weeks / But bears it out even to the edge of doom." In a lasting relationship, we may no longer be sick with desire every time we set eyes on the person we love, but this does not mean that many happily married people do not yearn for each other when parted, or continue to find each other sexually exciting. Still less does it mean that sentiment fades with the initial exuberant sensuality.

The ideals advocated by modern psychologists usually include: sexual equality, compatible interests, freedom from envy, mutual respect, acceptance of separate identities. Qualities such as these, together with the tenderness of a couple who have loved each other with real passion, and not forgotten it, provide the true ingredients of lasting love. The challenge and adventure of love do not end when lovers marry.

The ecstasy experienced early in a relationship is portrayed in Gustav Klimt's *The Kiss*. Its memory may act as a bond after initial passion has faded.

LOST LOVE

As soon as we fall in love we become vulnerable to – and peculiarly defenceless against – its loss. This is one of the risks we take for love: that the person in whom we have invested so many of our hopes and dreams, and so much longing, may go away, or fall out of love with us, or leave us for someone else, or be separated from us by some malign fate, or be mistakenly left by us – or even die.

Lost love, remembered and regretted, is the greatest theme of opera and popular music. Puccini's opera *La Bohème* dramatizes the fears of all lovers – that passionate love cannot last and that we may suffer the agony of watching the beloved die before our eyes.

In a sense, all lost love is a kind of death. What we feel is a grief as real as

During the Renaissance Ariadne, who married the god Dionysus, became a symbol of the restoration of life through death.

any caused by actual death, often sharpened to an unendurable pitch by the fact that all of our senses are involved – our whole being is missing the warmth, closeness and intimate delight of another loved body. Losing our love to another is acutely painful, and can lead to lingering bitterness if we let it. Yet if we are able to overcome such possessiveness, the experience of losing in love may also mature us – and be a preparation for something more lasting.

Lost Love

The loneliness and despair that we feel on losing a loved one is vividly evoked in this painting by Emma Turpin.

Shall I compare thee to a summer's day?
Thou art more lovely and more temperate:
Rough winds do shake the darling buds of May,
And summer's lease hath all too short a date:
Sometime too hot the eye of heaven shines,
And often is his gold complexion dimmed;
And every fair from fair sometime declines,
By chance, or nature's changing course, untrimmed;
But thy eternal summer shall not fade,
Nor lose possession of that fair thou owest,
Nor shall death brag thou wander'st in his shade,
When in eternal lines to time thou growest;
So long as men can breathe, or eyes can see,
So long lives this, and this gives life to thee.

WILLIAM SHAKESPEARE (1564–1616), Sonnet 18

THE LANGUAGE OF LOVE

Love hath a language of his own
A voice that goes
From heart to heart – whose mystic tone
Love only knows.

ANON, PERSIAN LOVE POEM

The language of love is largely private and unspoken. A lingering look, a touch, the answering pressure of a hand, can speak more directly than words. Ordinary language can seem desperately short of the emotional intensity that lovers feel.

This is perhaps why lovers have always found other ways to communicate – more individual, more personal, and often mysterious to anyone else. Only lovers really understand the emotional charge that lies behind a book or piece of music sent from one to the other, a memento, keepsake, ring, or flower.

THE LOOK OF LOVE

The eyes are the most immediate and powerful communicators of our emotions. It is almost impossible to mistake the feelings that they convey. Medieval writers believed that the process of falling in love began with the meeting of eyes, which they called the windows of the soul. They thought that a mystical transfusion found its way to the heart, producing the sensation of love by an almost alchemical reaction.

The Look of Love

Helen of Troy, the most beautiful woman in the world, is shown here gazing at her husband Menelaus.

We learn to appreciate and respond to the look of love almost from the time that we are born. Babies will search their mother's face until they focus on her eyes – and then smile, reassured by the glow of love they find there. Lovers almost become lost in each other's gaze, often oblivious to the smiles of the outside world. The eyes express love both consciously and unconsciously: dilated pupils, for example, are a classic signal of sexual arousal and eye make-up continues to be a major weapon in the battery of allure.

Spanish women, the inheritors of Moorish veils, were said to be able to play more games with their eyes than conjurors could with a pack of cards. In their ever-shifting language of flirtation, men might take a sideways movement of the eyes as a question, a blank stare as suffering, a wink as joy, an inward look as refusal, touched eyelids as a warning and lowered lids as consent. The most thrilling look was the sidelong "flash of lightning".

However, the look of love has no guarantee – an essential part of its charm. Everything can be said with the eyes, but nothing can be proven, as Stendhal was to observe: "Glances are the big guns of the virtuous coquette; everything can be conveyed in a look, and yet that look can always be denied."

The painting overleaf by Emma Turpin conveys the powerful attraction that can be aroused by even a casual glance.

The Look of Love

PUBLIC AND PRIVATE

Public and Private

"They love indeed who quake to say they love," wrote the most famous soldier-poet of the 16th century, Sir Philip Sidney. Declaring love for the first time has never been easy. Even if we believe that our love is returned, we may not immediately want to share our secret with the world.

The urge to shout love from the rooftops conflicts with a feeling that making it public in some way diminishes its mystic intensity. This instinctive reticence was almost a rule of love in some earlier societies. Courtly love was usually secretive, and André le Chapelain's 13th-century *Rules of Love* advised that "a love divulged seldom lasts". This reflected the codes of a time when the penalties for unsanctioned love were very high, and disclosure could bring down hostility, opposition, shame or complete social ruin on those involved.

We are far less secretive now, yet the change may be more superficial than it

Public and Private

first seems. Love still moves as it has always done between private and public worlds, testing the limits of each. Lovers still walk into the ordinary world carrying the secrets of their own extraordinary and sensual intimacy. However, the wider world has continued to provide the moral and social context into which love must fit if it is not to remain completely selfish – and in the end become claustrophobic.

In the 18th century, Venice was famous for its *ridottos*, or masked dancing parties. This detail from a painting by Pietro Longhi shows a pair of lovers flirting in the safety of their disguise.

THE MUSIC OF LOVE

The Music of Love

Love songs have for centuries provided a highly eloquent and flexible language of love. They can touch and move us in a way that cuts completely across the usual boundaries of age, social milieu or aesthetic taste – as even the ultra-sophisticated Noël Coward noted when he wrote in *Private Lives*: "Strange how potent cheap music is."

In Europe and the Middle East, love songs were traditionally performed by men. This late 18th-century painting depicts a Persian musician.

The power of music, and its ability to celebrate love, dominates the ancient Greek myth of Orpheus. Following the death of his adored wife Eurydice, the musician-poet descends into the depths of the Underworld to rescue her, enchanting the cold heart of Hades, the God of the Dead, with the songs of his enduring love.

In the musical salons of 7th-century Medina, beautiful, long-haired youths are believed to have played lutes and sung the praises of love as the very essence of life. In the 11th century the troubadour poets brought the tradition of courtly love to Europe, and music became seen as an essential ingredient of a secular love celebrated as the origin of virtue.

Love songs are more, however, than Sigmund Romberg's tender definition: "just a caress set to music". Folk ballads, country music, torch songs and rock songs all tell stories about lovers whose emotions everyone can identify with. The lyrics of countless love songs, from operatic arias or Schubert's delicate *Lieder* to the ultimate simplicity of the Beatles' "Love, love me do!", create infinite variations on the theme of love.

In *The Duet*, a watercolour by the 18th-century artist Thomas Rowlandson, a young couple are seen making music in an elegant English drawing room.

The Music of Love

THE DANCE OF LOVE

This wondrous myracle did Love devise
For Daucing is Love's proper exercise.
SIR JOHN DAVIES (1569–1626),
"ORCHESTRA: A POEM OF DAUNCING"

Dance is courtship in full flight. Its permitted embrace has long been the most openly erotic flirtation ritual, and has consequently often been attacked by the moral guardians of society. Many formal dances, such as those popular in 19th-century English assembly rooms, allowed little physical contact between the partners. Emotion could be conveyed only by shared, sidelong glances, lowered eyes and murmured conversation, for the dance floor was one of the few places where chaperoned young ladies had a chance to speak to men directly and alone.

At balls women were provided with dance cards on which to record their partners' names. These were prized as souvenirs long after the event itself. Ladies were encouraged to select several partners; to dance with the same man more than twice was to risk censure.

The most criticized dance of all was the waltz, in which couples circled the floor together, clasped in a close embrace. The dance swept across Europe in the early 1800s and soon crossed the Atlantic, prompting a flood of sermons and articles, as well as a tongue-in-cheek poem by Byron. Yet dancing never stopped, perhaps because no one can forget their

The waltz caused outrage when it was first introduced, but it became wildly popular.

own dancing days – celebrated even by the cynical Byron: "On with the dance! let joy be unconfined / No sleep till morn, when youth and pleasure meet / To chase the glowing hours with flying feet."

Every society through history has used the sensual power of dance, whether to delight the gods or simply the other sex. In the Bible, for example, the sexual charge of Salome's dance for King Herod secured her the head of John the Baptist as a reward. Bizet's tempestuous heroine Carmen exploits the tantalizing art of gypsy flamenco to ensnare her lovers José and Escamillo the bullfighter. In the 1920s, flamboyant performances of the popular Charleston became the hallmark of the emancipated "flapper".

Dancing has not lost its power in courtship. Prom dances in America and débutante balls in Europe are events as momentous as great aristocratic balls once were. The rituals of amorous smiles and suggestive movements continue to link dancing with courtship and love.

THE FOODS OF LOVE

The imagery of love and food is deeply intermingled, as both the anticipation and the experience of each carries a powerful sensual charge. Sexual love and desire are often described as being an unquenchable physical thirst or appetite, which may remain tantalizingly unfulfilled or be indulged to excess.

This sumptuous painting depicts an actual banquet held at the Ca Rezzonico, Venice, in September 1755. Such occasions of great festivity were enlivened by exotic foods and flirtation.

The thoughtful preparation of a meal for a loved one is consequently filled with great romantic significance. The hero of Ben Jonson's play *Volpone* promises to create for his love a meal of extraordinary rarity: "The heads of parrots, tongues of nightingales / The brains of peacocks and ostriches / Shall

The Foods of Love

be our food: and could we get the phoenix, / Though nature lost her kind, she were our dish."

Love-potions, magical birds and the reputedly great aphrodisiac powers of raw oysters may or may not serve to augment love, as popular myth would have us believe. Yet the real intimacy of shared food is both the perfect prelude to lovers' encounters and a powerful part in our nostalgic memories of them. Edwin Morgan's "Strawberries" recalls

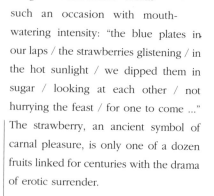

such an occasion with mouth-watering intensity: "the blue plates in our laps / the strawberries glistening / in the hot sunlight / we dipped them in sugar / looking at each other / not hurrying the feast / for one to come ..." The strawberry, an ancient symbol of carnal pleasure, is only one of a dozen fruits linked for centuries with the drama of erotic surrender.

The European colonization of Africa, Asia and the Americas resulted in the import of many unfamiliar foods. Several of these were believed to have aphrodisiac properties.

A. Yndia en trage de gala.
B. Yndia del Campo con su Arba Pacal
C. Arbol de Aguacates, y su Fruta.
D. Arbol de Chuimaicones con su Fruta en-
   tera, y partida.
E. Arbol de Chamburos con su Fruta en-
   tera, y abierta.
F. Mamey con sus ojas, y fruta abierta

A. Yndio Principal de
   Juesto trage de Gala.
B. Arbol de Guabas, Cachenorias, y
   Azigalillos.
C. Taigos Fruta, y el modo como se entra en
   su rama.
D. Arbol, y fruta delos Guayabos.
E. Yndio del Campo.

*Come live with me and be my
love
And we will all the pleasures
prove
That valleys, groves, hills, and
fields,
Woods, or steepy mountain
yields.*

*And we will sit upon the rocks,
Seeing the shepherds feed their
flocks,
By shallow rivers to whose falls
Melodious birds sing madrigals.*

*And I will make thee beds of
roses
And a thousand fragrant
posies,
A cap of flowers, and a kirtle
Embroidered all with leaves of
myrtle;*

*A gown made of the finest wool
Which from our pretty lambs
we pull;
Fair lined slippers for the cold,
With buckles of the purest gold;*

A belt of straw and ivy buds,
With coral clasps and amber
studs:
And if these pleasures may thee
move,
Come live with me, and be my
love.

The shepherds' swains shall
dance and sing
For thy delight each May
morning:
If these delights thy mind may
move,
Then live with me and be my
love.

CHRISTOPHER MARLOWE
(1564–93), "The Passionate
Shepherd to His Love"

CODED LOVE

Lovers have always had secrets to keep. Not saying exactly what you mean has been an ingredient of flirtation for centuries. If you have not made up your mind about someone, or suspect that they may not have made up their mind about you, a degree of conversational evasiveness is essential.

More serious codes have to be used to communicate love in situations in which discovery would be at best embarrassing, at worst dangerous. Writing love letters in invisible ink or secret codes are techniques that go back at least to Roman times. And throughout history, lovers have written coded messages to each other.

Such codes were usually simple ciphers with a pre-arranged key, but

Fans have been an instrument of flirtation for centuries.

Women writing letters, such as in this painting by Vermeer, were traditionally assumed to be writing to a lover.

Coded Love

Coded Love

the young Mozart found an original way around his father's ban on writing to an admirer by sending messages to "my beautiful English rose" in which musical notes were substituted for letters of the alphabet. Another popular technique was the suggestive use of literary or

---

THEY WHO ARE NEAR TO ME

They who are near to me do not know that
you are nearer to me than they are.
They who speak to me do not know that my heart
is full with your unspoken words.
They who crowd in my path do not know that
I am walking alone with you.
They who love me do not know that their love
brings you to my heart.

RABINDRANATH TAGORE (1861–1941)

mythological allusions. The French queen Marie Antoinette left novels with passages underlined for her courtiers to find.

However, it was precisely the arts employed to conceal meaning that enabled the writer's heart to speak directly to its true recipient – a paradox still relished by lovers today.

Stanley Spencer's *Love Letters* shows a man overwhelmed by the quantity – or perhaps by the content – of the notes that he and his lover are exchanging.

Cards have been exchanged by generations of lovers on St Valentine's Day.

This early 19th-century Swiss automaton snuff box would have been an extravagant token of love.

VALENTINES

The St Valentine's Day custom of lovers pledging themselves to each other is centuries old, though its association with two early Saints Valentine remains a mystery. A plausible origin of the tradition is suggested by Chaucer's 14th-century *Parlement of Foules*, which linked the saints' day on February 14 with the mating of birds – and, by extension, humans: "For this was on Seynt Valentynes day / When ev'ry fowl cometh to chese his make." The notion of a selection of partners on February 14 may have grown out of this symbolism of early spring.

In the 16th and 17th centuries in England, tradition permitted women to

select their valentines, by lot or by chance (for example, the first man sighted in the morning). A gift would then be expected from him in return.

Valentines

The practice of sending coded Valentine cards did not become established until the 19th century. It started in England and soon became highly popular in the United States. Valentine cards exploited the contemporary devotion to a secret language of flowers, in which illustrations of forget-me-nots, violets and roses spelt out whole paeans of feeling in complicated floral ciphers. Protected by anonymity, both men and women were able to take the initiative in

This mock $50 bill from the Bank of True Love was made in the USA in around 1850. It is an early example of the novelty card.

Floral messages on 19th-century cards were charged with meaning. Lily of the valley and forget-me-nots, for example, symbolized a pure and steadfast love.

declaring their love. "Never sign a valentine with your own name," was Sam Weller's advice to his master in Dickens' *Pickwick Papers*.

The endearments exchanged on our modern St Valentine's Day are just as elaborate and obscure. Six hundred years after Chaucer, the sexes still keep their annual appointment with each other, and mark St Valentine's Day with a variety of imaginative, entertaining and enduring rituals.

MESSAGES IN FLOWERS

Why is it no one ever sent me yet
One perfect limousine, do you suppose?
Ah no, it's always just my luck to get
One perfect rose.

DOROTHY PARKER (1893–1967), "ONE PERFECT ROSE"

Poppies' bright, warm colours have always held a particular charm for lovers.

Parker may have mocked the present of a single rose, but its power as an ambassador of love still transcends the cliché. Flowers have been emblems of secular and religious love for centuries. The word "posy", for example, which now means a small bunch, originally referred to a message of love, a piece of "poesy" (poetry), symbolized by the flowers themselves.

As gardens developed in medieval Europe, flowers were given symbolic meanings. The audiences at Shakespeare's *Hamlet* would have understood the resonances in Ophelia's speech to Laertes: "There is rosemary, that's for remembrance – pray you love, remember – and there is pansies, that's for thoughts."

Messages in Flowers

Messages in Flowers

However, it was not until the 19th century that these popular associations were formalized into an elaborate, secret language in which flowers were able to convey desires and sentiments that could not be openly expressed. More than just a parlour game, the code was based on the philosophical belief that truths could be expressed in natural forms.

In this Indian miniature, the god Krishna presents Radha with a lotus flower, symbol of fertility, sexuality, birth, rebirth and purity.

Messages in Flowers

TOKENS OF LOVE

Mark Antony may have pledged his kingdom for Cleopatra, but lovers have usually been content with smaller proofs of esteem. The long history of love's tokens and keepsakes reveals a bewildering range of objects, often trifling in themselves but all seeking to measure – and test – the power of love.

Keepsakes are in some

This painting by Emma Turpin has resonances of Cinderella.

ways expressions of the doubts as much as the certainties that exist in human relationships. The value invested in a

Tokens of Love

keepsake by the recipient is proof of regard for the giver – and such emotional significance may far exceed any material worth. Almost any small object might be pressed into service, from the purely pleasing (the solemnly worked pincushion of a 19th-century sailor) to the heavily symbolic, such as a lock of hair, implying a lover's surrender to the other. Early in his foreign travels, the young Lord Byron described how he had exchanged locks of hair with a "Spanish belle" at their parting. Regarding hers (which was about 3 feet

in length) as something of an encumbrance, he sensibly sent it back to his mother in England.

Young lovers in ancient Greece hung wreaths on their sweethearts' doors as a sign of affection.

The clasped hands on this early 19th-century gold bracelet are an ancient symbol. Once representing a legal contract, it came to mean faith and love.

Tokens of Love

Two hearts pierced by Cupid's arrow have become an international symbol of love. This lacquer box comes from Olimala in Mexico.

Keepsakes were particularly popular when couples were parted by long absences, and objects were often chosen for their intimate connection with a person's body. A full list of the kinds of keepsakes a medieval woman might expect, in consolation for the travels of her roving knight, appeared in André le Chapelain's popular *Rules of Love* of the 13th century: " … a handkerchief, a fillet for the hair, a wreath of gold or silver, a breastpin, a mirror or a girdle, a purse, a tassel, a comb, sleeves, gloves … any little gift useful for the care of the person, or pleasing to look at."

The keepsake could, of course, be a prelude to love, as well as confirmation of it. In Shakespeare's *A Midsummer Night's Dream*, the spurned lover Egeus accuses his rival of having captured Hermia's heart by stealing "the impression of her fantasy / With bracelets of thy hair, rings, gawds, conceits, knacks, trifles, nosegays, sweetmeats ..." The desire to surprise a loved one with an unexpected present is a classic, never entirely altruistic, symptom of love. Perfumes, jewelry, books and items of clothing have been traditional favourites, as have gifts of music, from a single, poignant serenade to the latest, enduring CD. Even ephemeral items of food can play a significant role. Cleopatra, for example, was said to have ordered a wild boar to be roasted every hour in case her Antony should return.

The course of modern love is still punctuated with tokens and keepsakes, perhaps because the need to prove and reiterate love is stronger than ever. A particular present from a lover, or simply something he or she once wore, can be invested with almost talismanic properties. Nor should we forget that the photograph in a wallet or pocketbook is only the modern form of the miniature portraits that have been exchanged by lovers through the centuries.

The heart shape has become synonymous with the word love, often replacing it on T-shirts and bumper stickers.

Is love a light for me? A steady light,
A lamp within whose pallid pool I dream
Over old love-books? Or is it a gleam,
A lantern coming towards me from afar
Down a dark mountain? Is my love a star?
Ah me! – so high above so coldly bright!

The fire dances. Is my love a fire
Leaping down the twilight muddy and bold?
Nay, I'd be frightened of him. I'm too cold
For quick and eager loving. There's a gold
Sheen on these flower petals as they fold
More truly mine, more like to my desire.

The flower petals fold. They are by the sun
Forgotten. In a shadowy wood they grow
Where the dark trees keep up a to-and-fro
Shadowy waving. Who will watch them shine
When I have dreamed my dream? Ah,
        darling mine,
Find them, gather them for me one by one.

KATHERINE MANSFIELD *(1888–1923),*
"Secret Flowers"

She walks in beauty, like the night
Of cloudless climes and starry skies;
And all that's best of dark and bright
Meet in her aspect and her eyes:
Thus mellowed to that tender light
Which heaven to gaudy day denies.

One shade the more, one ray the less,
Had half impaired the nameless grace
Which waves in every raven tress,
Or softly lightens o'er her face;
Where thoughts serenely sweet express
How pure, how dear their dwelling place.

And on that cheek, and o'er that brow,
So soft, so calm, yet eloquent,
The smiles that win, the tints that glow,
But tell of days in goodness spent,
A mind at peace with all below,
A heart whose love is innocent!

LORD BYRON *(1788–1824),*
"She Walks in Beauty"

An illuminated panel from the *Book of Hours of Charles of Angoulême*.

The 18th-century aristocracy loved to conduct flirtations dressed as Arcadian shepherds and shepherdesses.

COURTSHIP

The complicated and ever-shifting rules of Western courtship have always been based on the reasonable suspicion that when a man sets out to capture a woman's heart his primary motive is sex and not love. Courtship is essentially a way of putting men's declarations of love to the test.

Courtship traditions go back to the 12th century, when the nobility of southern France, modelling themselves on Arabic and Moorish ideals, began to develop the arts of courtly love. This new romantic fashion was partly an elegant piece of theatre, a delightful pastime for bored wives and temporarily idle young men. Court ladies could practise their skills of flirtation without committing themselves to the risks of conducting

an illicit affair, while their male "vassals" could show off their charm. Notions of secular love as a gentle feminine tyranny, a test of men's virtue and a life-enhancing experience have permeated most romantic literature ever since.

As courtship came to be seen as a prelude to marriage, the

process changed to one of establishing a man's social and economic suitability. In prosperous 19th-century society, courtship etiquette became extremely formal.

When Western couples began to select and marry partners for love, new rules of courtship gradually emerged. This could be seen most clearly in the United States, where the tests of love were increasingly conducted in private rather than in public. American love

In this detail from Goya's *The Parasol*, a demure young woman is shielded from the sun by a servant. Her sidelong glance and upheld fan suggest that she is an accomplished flirt.

Courtship

letters from the 19th century reveal repeated sequences of doubt, trial and reassurance as women tested men's professions of love by placing one obstacle after another in their path. This process of emotional assessment, foreshadowed in Jane Austen's novels, established modern rules of courtship.

In the West today, dating and courting are conducted far more informally than they were even as recently as the 1950s. Yet where love is concerned, true bonding still requires a passage through some process of emotional trial and judgment. The difference in modern relationships – and it is a huge one – is that men and women now increasingly test each other on an equal basis.

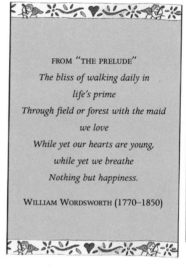

FROM "THE PRELUDE"
*The bliss of walking daily in
life's prime
Through field or forest with the maid
we love
While yet our hearts are young,
while yet we breathe
Nothing but happiness.*

WILLIAM WORDSWORTH (1770–1850)

THE PROPOSAL

Among all love's rituals, the most awesome is the proposal of marriage. This instant is more powerfully charged than even the act of marriage itself, and its timing and setting assume an enduring significance. The proposal demands a daring leap of faith, since it cannot be tested in advance – nor can it be undone once spoken. Nowhere else in a relationship is one person so vulnerable, with all future hopes and plans depending on the outcome.

The proposal is primarily an emotional drama of the West, as Eastern conventions of arranged marriages rely on couples developing their love after the engagement, rather than before. Many Western traditions have their roots in 19th-century proposals, in which nervous lovers, who were often relative strangers, inched across the gap between them. The agonizing uncertainty tended to be reflected in broken sentences or

The Proposal

This illustration, from a 1921 fashion magazine, is entitled *Oui!* It captures the moment at a dance when the two beautifully dressed lovers agree to marry.

The Proposal

In this painting
of a betrothal,
a blindfolded
Cupid prepares
to fire an arrow
of love at the
princess. Other
suitors watch
apprehensively
for her response.

The Proposal

clumsy avowals, such as the gruff decla-
ration of love "Barkis is willin'" in Charles
Dickens' novel *David Copperfield*.

Of course, not all proposals
succeed. Sometimes the stresses of the
moment can prove overwhelming and
the words remain unspoken. One of the
most poignant scenes in literature occurs
in *Anna Karenina*, when Kozynyshev,
suddenly determined to propose to
Varenka, despite his pledge of loyalty to
a former, dead lover, approaches her in
the woods. He knows that she is expect-
ing a proposal, " ... but instead of those
words some perverse reflection caused
him to ask: 'What is the difference
between a white boletus and a birch
mushroom?'" Each recognizes that the
crucial moment has been irrevocably
lost and cannot now ever be regained.

Modern proposals, often based on a
much greater intimacy, still present lovers
with a challenge. Despite our supposed
sophistication, the proposal remains a
moment of exquisite awkwardness.

THE RING

The ring is one of the most ancient forms of love token. Originally used as the seal and emblem of authority, it is also a unique symbol of completeness, eternity and union. The Romans' early betrothal rings, which were made of iron, were designed in the shape of two clasped hands to signify the exchange of legal vows. The first Christian wedding rings, which appeared around 860CE, are believed to have been worn originally on the fingers of the right hand.

In *The Measure for the Wedding Ring*, a fiancé lovingly checks the size of his beloved's ring finger.

The most common form of wedding ring – a plain gold band – dates back to Celtic times. Its classic simplicity has been increasingly favoured over more

The Ring

showy versions, while the symbolic constancy of gold has become an established emblem of enduring love.

Engagement rings and other forms of love jewelry have traditionally afforded more elaborate expressions of love, especially in Renaissance Europe, where rings contained bezels that hid tiny hearts or other romantic keepsakes. The 16th-century jemmel ring was composed of interlocking sections, which couples broke apart on betrothal. They then

This portrait of *Marsilio and his Wife*, by the 16th-century Italian artist Lorenzo Lotto, depicts the betrothal of a wealthy young bourgeois couple. Cupid, the god of love, watches with much satisfaction as a ring is placed on the girl's finger.

symbolically reassembled the ring as a token of love on their wedding day.

A rich, widely understood language of jewels invested the stones of a ring with huge significance. Each was integrally linked to the nature of love: ruby for ardour, emerald for sincerity, garnet for constancy, amethyst for Venus and a diamond for the incorruptibility of marriage. The enduring quality of diamonds also rendered them a natural choice for the eternity ring, a pledge of commitment after marriage and often associated with the birth of children.

Yet perhaps the rings of greatest significance to their owners are those secretly cherished but never displayed. These are often charged with memories of a love lost through death or circumstance. After his death, the English king William of Orange was found to be wearing on a ribbon the gold wedding ring that he had given Princess Mary, still entwined with a lock of her hair.

The Ring

The Wedding

THE WEDDING

Only in the 20th century did the question arise of whether the traditional wedding has anything to do with the language of love. In the West, where love is increasingly viewed as a private affair, the more elaborate rituals of marriage may seem irrelevant to a highly personal emotion. Yet a traditional wedding still captures our imagination, and without doubt it remains the most evocative spectacle in the drama of love.

Wedding presents, such as this 18th-century Greek cushion cover, are traditionally important gifts. They bring good wishes for future prosperity into the couple's new home.

For thousands of years, marriage has been a formal rite of passage. Earlier societies, to whom order in human society was inseparable from a greater natural harmony, imbued marriage rites with a sacred significance because they seemed to affirm the continuation of life itself. Fertility symbols are present in marriage rituals from very diverse cultures. Among the many examples still found in a traditional Western wedding are tossing the bridal bouquet and showering the couple with confetti. In modern Japan, many weddings continue to be solemnized by Shinto priests, or *kannushi*, reflecting the ancient religion's close associations with fertility and renewal.

Even in a secular context, the language of marriage vows is solemn. Although

The Wedding

This woodcut by Eric Gill shows a couple locked in a close embrace. Together they form a heart.

FROM "THE BRIDE"
At last the world says yes;
It wishes me roses and sons.
My friends stand shyly at the door,
Carrying love gifts.

Chemises in cellophane,
Plates, flowers, lace ...
They kiss my cheeks, they marvel
I'm to be a wife.

BELLA AKHMADULINA, TRS FROM
THE RUSSIAN BY STEPHAN STEPANCHEV

The Wedding

the styles of weddings have varied widely to reflect the values of individual societies, their intention remains essentially the same. The union of a couple is surrounded with as much social, religious, magical and legal pomp and circumstance as possible. The laws, duties, vows and customs of these incurably optimistic ceremonies were all designed to make the marriage permanent as well as fruitful – although, sadly, we all know the inconsistencies of the human heart.

The best weddings are personal rather than formulaic, welcoming

families and friends into shared happiness. The creation of new and delightful forms is a tribute to the human powers of love and imagination.

Botticelli's *The Wedding Feast* shows men and women seated at opposite tables.

Archetypes of Love

Out flew the web and floated wide;
The mirror cracked from side to side.
ALFRED LORD TENNYSON (1809–92),
"THE LADY OF SHALOTT"

According to Carl Jung's theory of the collective unconscious, we inherit cultural archetypes that influence the human psyche because they embody desires and anxieties that remain more or less constant. Countless archetypal stories dramatize and resolve love's key temptations and challenges.

There are, of course, dangers in becoming spellbound by the archetype. Tennyson's Lady of Shalott was forbidden to do more than weave images reflected in a mirror. When she turned to look directly at the handsome Lancelot, her idealized world was shattered.

THE GOD OF LOVE

The god of love, Eros, was first described by the Greek poet Hesiod in the 8th century BCE. One of the earliest gods to emerge from Chaos (according to Hesiod's *Theogany*), Eros was a fundamental principle of life: an inexorable, amoral desire for all things to mingle: "the most beautiful of all the immortal gods, who loosens the limbs and overcomes judgment and wise counsel in the breasts of gods and all humans."

To the Greeks, Eros represented the strength and urgency of love, rather than its delicate sensuality and pleasure. These qualities formed the feminine essence of Aphrodite, who featured as the primary deity of love in the great poems of Homer. Plato's *Symposium* reinvested Eros with his original authority, but sought to distinguish his spiritual impact from human sexual passion. The god represented a highly refined and transcendent love, an imaginative ideal

Bronzino's *An Allegory with Venus and Cupid* depicts the debased god of love as a knowing adolescent, engaged in sensual play with his mother. The painting forms a 16th-century warning of the perils of erotic promiscuity.

The God of Love

The Roman goddess of love, Venus, was held to be Cupid's mother. He shared her power over human emotions.

that has continued to both fascinate and perplex lovers ever since.

Eros later became associated more with the lightning process of "falling in love". An image of cause rather than effect, he was equipped with a bow and arrows of irresistible desire and subsumed into Roman mythology as Venus's son Cupid. No longer a primary creative force, the god of love was often presented as a mischievous boy, loosing off arrows of infatuation without a thought for the feelings of those he wounded. Wilful

Cupid was notorious for his lack of discrimination, reflecting a vision of falling in love as an entirely random process. His arbitrariness was often symbolized in medieval art by a blindfold. The "blind bow-boy" from Shakespeare's *Romeo and Juliet* became a widely accepted image for a rather heartless, cruel and amoral sexual imperative.

GODDESSES OF LOVE

Goddesses of love are a concept even older than Eros, and have appeared in many mythological forms. Their earliest manifestations were as fertility deities, aspects of the Earth Mother from whom all life derived. The savagery of nature

From Hellenistic times, the Greek god of love, Eros, became subservient to the goddess Aphrodite. He was usually depicted as a mischievous boy.

Goddesses of Love

MADRIGAL 52

Diana, naked in the shadowy pool,
Brought no more rapture to the greedy eyes
Of him who watched her splashing in the cool
Than did my glimpse of a maiden unaware
Washing a snood, the gossamer garment of
My lady's wild and lovely golden hair;
Wherefore, although the sky burnt hot above,
I shake and shiver with a chill of love.

FRANCESCO PETRARCH (1304–74),
TRS FROM THE ITALIAN
BY MORRIS BISHOP

Goddesses of Love

was often reflected in the dual roles of ancient goddesses: Ishtar in Sumeria and Astarte in Phoenicia were associated with war as well as with the planet Venus and love.

The world's first love poetry was probably inspired by the Egyptian goddess Hathor. She represented the gentle, creative power of love and fertility. Greek mythology refined aspects of earlier deities in the enchanting Aphrodite, the enduring archetype of sensual love. Her complex, contradictory character reflected the moods and emotions experienced in, and aroused by, love. In an alternative guise, as Aphrodite Pandemos, she was married to Hephaestus, the smith of the gods, who symbolized the creative intellect. This version

Botticelli's *The Birth of Venus* portrays one version of the goddess's origin – that she was born from sea foam and washed ashore at Paphos.

of Aphrodite represented the more sexual aspects of love, implicit in her origins as a fertility deity. Both earthly and celestial, her quixotic nature epitomized the wanton fluctuations of love.

Aphrodite, who became known to the Romans as Venus, is Homer's "sweet and winning goddess" – but she is also jealous and unfaithful. She owns a magic girdle of enticement, yet when she falls in love with the beautiful youth Adonis, and discovers that he is immune to its magic, she reveals herself as possessive and demanding. The goddess has been the archetype of female beauty ever since the 4th century BCE when the sculptor Praxiteles created the sensuous *Cnidian Aphrodite*. Attended by the Three Graces, her gentle and smiling handmaidens, she is anything but gentle in her treatment of mortals who have offended her. She punishes Hippolytus for worshipping her rival, Artemis, by making his stepmother, Phaedra, fall disastrously in love with him.

Goddesses of Love

Love and Magic

The powerful impact of love has always seemed magical in its blinding suddenness and intensity. Romantics through the generations have wanted to believe that their love is somehow predetermined or ordained. Once lovers could no longer place their faith in Cupid or the gods of love, they chose astrology, magic or fate – the Arab *kismet* – to give their choices mystical confirmation.

A sorceress weaves a love spell in a 15th-century German painting, *The Magic of Love*.

Literature tells us again and again that love's tragedies are predestined. In the great medieval love cycle of Tristan and Isolde, as Tristan brought Isolde to her wedding with his uncle and lord, King

Mark of Cornwall, the unhappy couple were accidentally served a magic love potion intended for the future husband and wife. Instead, it bound Tristan and Isolde in guilty love, treachery, anguished separations and eventual death. The fatal potion is a metaphor for the overwhelming impact of love and desire.

Folklore and fairytales also seek to provide magical explanations for love's mysteries. Unconscious or conscious desires have always been expressed in stories of sorcery, enchantment, shapechanging and the breaking of physical laws. Events in these tales, full of psychological significance, unfold as in a dream, where we fall in love or are loved with startling ease.

Love at first sight may be a magical transformation or a delusion. Shakespeare mocks its effect in *A Midsummer Night's Dream* when Oberon claims that the juice of the flower called love-in-idleness, rubbed on the eyelids, "Will make or man or woman madly dote

/ Upon the next live creature that it sees". Titania's ensuing passion for Bottom the weaver, magically endowed with an ass's head, parodies the delusions of lovers ensnared by passion.

The secular, sceptical, modern age retains its fascination with love and magic. Whether seeking compatibility in the signs of the Zodiac or using the traditional powers of herbs to reinvigorate desire, today's lovers continue to respond to the irrational power of love.

Gustav Klimt's painting *The Sea Serpent* portrays a woman ensnared in the embrace of a sea monster.

Love and Magic

The Power of Beauty

THE POWER OF BEAUTY

Beauty has always inspired a range of ambivalent feelings, from devotion to suspicion, anguish to delight. Its impact on the human imagination is enormous, investing the possessor with great emotional power.

The ancient Greek theory of Ideal Beauty has long dominated Western culture. Sir Frank Dicksee's portrait, *Miranda* (above), shows a 19th-century English lady dressed as a Greek goddess.

The potential danger of female beauty, as well as the passions it can inspire, is epitomized in myth by Helen of Troy. According to Homer's epic poem *The Iliad*, her loveliness provided the catalyst for a long, destructive war between Greece and Troy. The goddesses Aphrodite, Athene and Hera all claimed a 'golden apple dedicated to "the most beautiful", and were vain enough to submit

This Indian miniature (right) shows the god Krishna dazzled as Radha reveals her beautiful face.

to a beauty contest judged by the young Trojan prince Paris. Beset with tempting offers from each contender, Paris chose Aphrodite, the goddess of love, who promised to give him the most beautiful woman in the world. Aphrodite helped Paris to persuade Helen, the queen of Sparta, to abandon her husband and flee with Paris to Troy. After ten years of war, the avenging Greek fleets destroyed Troy and its inhabitants.

This ancient story is an epic metaphor for the ambivalent relationship of beauty and love, and the destruction that it can create within a marriage. Great beauty may inspire desire, jealousy or betrayal; it can provoke rivalry,

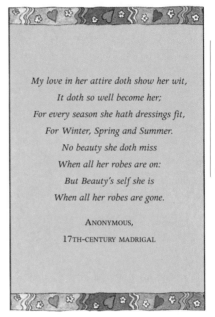

My love in her attire doth show her wit,
It doth so well become her;
For every season she hath dressings fit,
For Winter, Spring and Summer.
No beauty she doth miss
When all her robes are on:
But Beauty's self she is
When all her robes are gone.

ANONYMOUS,
17TH-CENTURY MADRIGAL

The Power of Beauty

Jupiter and Io by Antonio Correggio depicts the story of the beautiful priestess of Argos who was loved by Jupiter (Zeus). The god changed her into a heifer in an attempt to shield her from the envy of his wife Juno (Hera).

disharmony and war. Historically, the impact of beauty has turned politicians and soldiers from the path of duty and determined the fate of whole kingdoms and empires. "Had Cleopatra's nose been a little shorter, the whole face of the world might have been changed," wrote the French philosopher Blaise Pascal.

Pascal touches here on a truth about beauty – that its ultimately mysterious power can depend upon an irresistible detail. The power of both male and female beauty depends on personality, as well as on prevailing cultural and aesthetic fashions. We have only to compare the rounded stomachs, thin arms and small breasts of medieval beauties with Rubens' paintings of full-breasted, heavy-bodied goddesses to see that ideas of beauty change. What is constant about beauty is its desirability and the fascination it exerts over the beholder who feels its spell. "If ever any beauty I did see," wrote John Donne, "Which I desired and got / 'twas but a dream of thee."

The Power of Beauty

THE COURTESAN

In pre-Islamic Assyria, Persia and Egypt, most royal courts had a harem, consisting of the ruler's wife, concubines and attendants. The women often competed for power.

The courtesan might seem at first to represent the antithesis of love, but in many ways her history is spectacularly romantic. From the *hetairae* of ancient Greece to the powerful mistresses of 17th-century kings, courtesans have been the objects of idealized love and passion. Historically, many received the love that was absent from aristocratic marriages of convenience – though love was clearly not all that men sought in these liaisons.

The true courtesan was traditionally far more than a beautiful prostitute. In the Floating World of 17th-century Japan, the *oiran*, or senior courtesans, were highly educated women, expertly tutored in music and poetry, as well as in the arts of love-making. The Greek *hetairae* were permitted to mix socially with men and frequently held far more influence over them than did their wives. Xenophon, the Greek

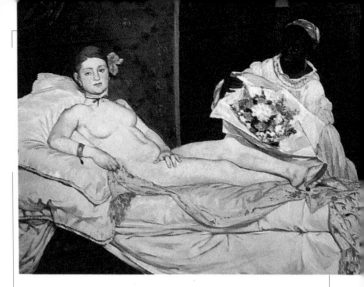

philosopher, claimed that the *hetaira* Diotima taught him what he knew of higher love, while another, Phryne, is cited by Plutarch as a renowned enchantress who inspired, among many others, the celebrated sculptor, Praxiteles.

Successful courtesans may have left abandoned wives – and in some societies their own husbands – in their wake, but these women often commanded intense love. Many of the most renowned courtesans in history were also cultured and sophisticated, enjoying considerable

Manet's painting *Olympia*, which depicts a prostitute and her black maid, caused a scandal when it was exhibited at the Paris Salon in 1865. The model's bold, provocative gaze challenged the viewer with an assertion of her confident sexuality.

An 18th-century print, *Lovers*, by the Japanese artist Kitagawa Utamaro. At the height of his career Utamaro produced prints of the concubines of Toyotomi Hideyoshi, the military ruler.

power and prestige. Roxelana Sultan, allegedly once a Russian slave, ended her 16th-century career by ruling the harem of Suleiman the Magnificent and advising the Ottoman ruler in his war against the Egyptian sultanate. Famous among the *cortegiane* of the Italian Renaissance was the poet Tullia d'Aragona, a woman whose philosophical writings engaged men's minds while her striking eyes captured their hearts. In France, extraordinary women such as La Pompadour and Diane de Poitiers captivated kings and used the power of love to influence the unfolding of history itself.

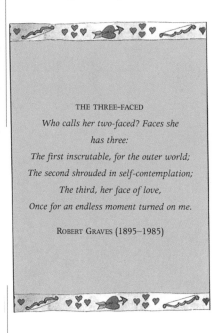

THE THREE-FACED

*Who calls her two-faced? Faces she
has three:
The first inscrutable, for the outer world;
The second shrouded in self-contemplation;
The third, her face of love,
Once for an endless moment turned on me.*

ROBERT GRAVES (1895–1985)

THE IMAGE OF DESIRE

The Image of Desire

This illustration
by Aubrey
Beardsley was
created for
Oscar Wilde's
Salome. The play
portrays Salome's
passion for John
the Baptist,
which becomes
murderous when
her ideal spurns
her love.

Discovering and falling in love with the man or woman of our dreams is not so common as we may wish to believe. Yet the search for a preconceived ideal attracts our imagination. If the ideal is not available, myths have often explored the possibility of creating it.

Ovid's story of Pygmalion describes the impulse to mould a love object to one's own desire. The sculptor Pygmalion, disgusted by the wanton behaviour of the women of Cyprus, had sworn never to marry. He poured his longing for a purer beauty into carving an ivory statue of a woman, and then fell desperately in love with his creation. Venus, the Roman goddess of love, took pity on him and brought the statue to life.

George Bernard Shaw's comedy of *Pygmalion* reinterpreted the fable in an early 20th-century context. Eliza Doolittle, a London flower-girl, is moulded into a splendid lady by the egotistical Professor Higgins. However, she finally informs him that she has outgrown his experiment and intends to make a life of her own. This psychologically convincing ending is characteristic of such love affairs. They frequently founder on the narcissism of the dominant partner, who only loves what he has created and resents any assertion of individual identity.

Modern images of desire are often film or pop stars. Redirecting our desire to a person in the everyday world is a significant stage in emotional development. Yet we are all Pygmalions to a degree: falling in love would be impossible without some conception of what we believe the other to be.

Jean-Léon Gérome's painting *Pygmalion and Galatea* captures the miraculous moment when the statue of Galatea comes to life and kisses her sculptor.

The Image of Desire

THE VIRGIN AND
THE UNICORN

A detail from a 15th-century tapestry (above) entitled *The Lady and the Unicorn*.

In medieval times, the unicorn was a metaphor for the Holy Spirit, while the lady represented the Virgin Mary (left).

The Virgin and the Unicorn

One of the paradoxes of deep human love is that it represents an imaginative synthesis of spiritual and sensual desires. For centuries, this apparent contradiction led Christian moralists to argue that all carnal love was sinful except as a means of procreation within lawful marriage.

Out of the struggle to reconcile sexuality with purity emerged the legend of the virgin and the unicorn. The medieval symbol of pure love was a beast of fable – a graceful white animal that resembled the oryx antelope of

The Virgin and the Unicorn

Arabia, with a spiral horn on its forehead, the maned head and body of a horse, the hoofs of an antelope and the tail of a lion. By the 15th century, when the famous group of tapestries of *The Lady and the Unicorn* were made for Jean le Viste, duc d'Arcy, the symbol had been elaborated into a complex allegory of spiritualized love. The sexual convention of the male hunting the desired female was reversed, and erotic love was sublimated into tenderness. The elusive and fierce unicorn with its phallic horn could be captured only by a virgin, in whose lap it would quietly rest its head.

At a secular level, the unicorn embodies male strength, freedom and virility. It submits to the maiden as the conventions of courtly love required the knight to surrender his heart and autonomy to his lady. However, at the heart of the fable is a more enduring idea: that goodness has an essential power over wildness, and that love can refine and control emotions as well as inflame them.

THE BEAST ADORED

One of the most poignant love stories ever written is the fable of Beauty and the Beast, made famous in the version by Madame Leprince de Beaumont in 1757. Its heroine agrees to enter a monster's castle as hostage for her father. The monster falls in love with her and begins to pine when she shrinks from him in horror. Finding him kind, and pitying his anguish, she eventually kisses him – to discover that he is really a fine prince.

The Beast is a recurrent feature of fairytales, where appearances are often set at variance with reality. In another manifestation he is the loathsome Frog

Zeus as a bull in Francesci's *The Rape of Europa* (above) and Henri Fuseli's *Europa and the Bull* (below).

The Beast Adored

Prince, able to escape from his repulsive outer skin only by the willingness of another to see beneath it. As the English moralist G. K. Chesterton perceived, the truth that such tales disclose "is that a thing must be loved before it is lovable". The power of the archetype lies in a universal longing to be loved for what we are, rather than how we appear.

Stories in which the Beast is animalistic have a different, more disturbing subtext. From the satyrs of Greek mythology onward, the Beast has been a recurring symbol of male lust, which may simultaneously attract and repel. The dark, brooding heroes of romantic fiction refine the archetype, but retain the power of its underlying sexuality.

FROM "LEDA AND THE SWAN"

A sudden blow: the great wings beating still
Above the staggering girl, her thighs caressed
By the dark webs, her nape caught in his bill,
He holds her helpless breast upon his breast.

How can those terrified vague fingers push
The feathered glory from her loosening thighs?
And how can body, laid in that white rush,
But feel the strange heart beating where it lies?

W. B. YEATS (1865–1939)

THE OBSTACLE

If there is one overriding message in all the writing on love, it is that achieving true love is a battle. Every lover, said Ovid, is a soldier, and love has always been considered a prize to be fought for. There are no couples in literature – or at least none whom we care to remember – who have not had to confront obstacles, sometimes terrible ones, in order to be together.

The love of Mars, the god of war, and Venus, the goddess of love, is depicted by Mantegna.

Recent history includes two powerful stories of love that provoked divided loyalties. On January 30, 1889, the young Archduke Rudolph, the Crown Prince of Austria, was found dead at his

The Obstacle

Possible parental deception is the subject of the painting *Trust Me* (above), by the Pre-Raphaelite artist Sir John Everett Millais.

Hero Awaiting the Return of Leander (left) by Evelyn de Morgan portrays the Greek priestess whose lover swam across the Hellespoint each night to visit her.

hunting lodge of Mayerling, shot by his own revolver. Beside him was the body of the Baroness Maria Vetsera, aged only 18. The Crown Prince appears to have chosen death rather than remain torn between his marriage and his love for Maria, and it seems that she chose to die with him. "Forgive me for what I have done," she wrote to her mother, "I could not resist love." No more, 50 years later, could the British king Edward VIII, enthralled by the American Wallis Simpson. In Britain a constitutional crisis ensued over his wish to marry a divorcee; Edward abdicated from the throne in 1936, to be free to marry Wallis and live with her abroad in self-imposed exile.

Modern lovers may not have to choose between their kingdoms and their love, and may rarely have occasion to risk death for each other. However, dramatic

The Obstacle

stories of lovers' obstacles continue to fascinate us, being idealizations of our own experience. We have all known the heightening of emotion when love is obstructed, and the irony that love often becomes clearly defined for us only after it has been somehow thwarted.

Literature has dramatized the trials of love in a myriad of different ways, from the metaphorical briar thickets that spring up in the path of suitors to the material impediments of money, or the constraints of social class (which separated Heathcliff from Cathy in *Wuthering Heights*). Differences of politics may also impinge on lovers: Boris Pasternak's novel *Dr Zhivago* describes the tragic division of Lara and Zhivago by the ideological hatreds of civil war following the Russian Revolution.

Opposition by parents has been a consistent theme in the trials of young lovers since Ovid's tale of Pyramus and Thisbe. These two lovers defy their parents by talking through a crack in the wall between their houses, before the mistaken belief that Thisbe is dead causes Pyramus to kill himself. The story of Romeo and Juliet, who are fatally divided by the family feuds of Montague and Capulet, has come to exemplify star-crossed lovers everywhere. Modern political or religious tensions have generated yet further occasions to illustrate this age-old theme. Emotional pressure to keep a child, particularly a daughter, at home may prove another obstacle to successful love. It can be exerted by a parent in a variety of subtle ways; for example Mr Woodhouse in Jane Austen's novel *Emma* falls ill with exquisite timing at the prospect of any situation that he might dislike.

Nevertheless, love continues to survive and even to thrive on its many obstacles. Young lovers still defy their parents to elope, or at least dream of it. However, other affairs are simply, and tragically, overwhelmed before they begin by the small misdirections of fate.

The Obstacle

THE PRISONER IN THE TOWER

The image of a beautiful woman imprisoned in a tower is a recurrent motif in art and literature. Carl Jung identified it as a fundamental psychological archetype. It symbolized for him every man's unconscious search for his *anima* – the female side of the male psyche. By falling in love, men sought to discover a projection of their *anima* – the princess in the tower.

However, the image also has a wider symbolism. The tower is perceived as a male emblem of ambition; in terms of love, it may also portray female purity and inaccessibility. In art, the woman in a tower or castle specifically symbolizes chastity.

In mythology, towers are linked with female chastity, either self-imposed or enforced by others – a state from which the heroine is usually rescued.

The Prisoner in the Tower

This Bengali painting shows a couple attempting to elope together on the back of an elephant.

In the great medieval allegory *The Romance of the Rose*, the lover had to attack the Castle of Love to pick his rosebud and achieve his heart's desire. In similar tales, the allegorical Castle of Love was often guarded by Jealousy.

The implication of the archetype was that the prisoner in the tower must wait passively for deliverance, rather than take any initiative herself. The modern adaptation of this idea is described in D. H. Lawrence's *The Rainbow*, where it reflects the growing maturity of the novel's heroine. Entranced as a girl by the story of Elaine, aloof from the world and loyally guarding Lancelot's shield, the adult Ursula has the confidence to leave her imaginary tower behind and, like a modern woman, go looking for love.

THE KNIGHT

In the classic 1942 film *Casablanca*, Humphrey Bogart (right) plays Rick, who saves the lives of his former lover and her husband.

Lancelot of the Lake, seen below capturing a castle, was the model of Arthurian chivalry and bravery.

The knight in shining armour has been one of the most enduring of all love archetypes – perhaps because it responds to certain desires in both women and men. Its greatest exemplar, Lancelot of the Lake, was as brave and adventurous as any man could wish to be. Yet he was also utterly ruled by love – so enthralled by Queen Guinevere that he would face any danger, accept any humiliation and betray any loyalty except to her.

Lancelot is a figure straight out of the courtly love traditions of 12th-century France. The lengthy poem by Chrétien de Troyes that celebrates his exploits was written under the patronage of a woman – Marie, Comtesse de Champagne. Thus the knight of romantic tradition, at least in his origins, was not simply the male power fantasy to which he is sometimes reduced – a conquering hero riding around rescuing damsels in distress. Lancelot's freedom of action was in fact deeply compromised by his love for Guinevere, the wife of his own lord. She was the controlling force in his life, and seems to have enjoyed her power, putting his love to rather cruel or arbitrary tests. "The knight departing for new adventures offends his lady, but she has nothing but contempt for him if he remains at her feet," observed Simone de Beauvoir.

The image of the knight has assumed many different forms since

FROM "GREEN SONG"
The naked Knight in the coat of mail
Shrieked like a bird that flees through
the leaves
The dark bird proud as the Prince of
the Air –
"I am the world's last love ... Beware"

EDITH SITWELL (1887–1964)

early medieval romances. Cervantes' novel *Don Quixote* parodies the unreal idealism of the knightly code through its charming but incompetent anti-hero. Nor was it solely a male preserve. The ambivalent figure of the female knight in Renaissance poetry exploited the contrast between steely armour and soft, milky limbs for a powerful erotic charge.

Paolo Uccello's *St George and the Dragon* depicts the patron saint of England slaughtering the dragon to release the captive maiden – a theme recurring in countless fairy-tales and myths.

The romantic figure of the male knight was much admired in the 19th century for his associated virtues of courage, honour and courtesy to the ladies in his charge. In Britain this was expressed in the work of Pre-Raphaelite painters, highly influenced by Arthurian legends, and of poets such as Alfred, Lord Tennyson. The passive role of women in many such tales — beautiful, imperilled, but dependent on a male to rescue and protect them — may reflect contemporary male unease about the growing demands of women for more economic and social freedom.

Nowadays the theme of rescue has begun to look archaic, as more equal relationships assume an ideal of mutual support and assistance. Yet as a figure of faithful love and resourceful courage, the knight is unlikely to disappear from romantic tradition. Who was the shadowy figure behind Humphrey Bogart in *Casablanca* or Gary Cooper in *High Noon* if not a modern knight errant?

GARDENS OF THE SENSES

The garden has presented lovers throughout history with an extraordinarily sensual setting. A real garden is already a world apart, an idealization of nature placed within a defining frame. Into this perfect romantic space, writers and artists have poured their complex, ambivalent allegories of Eden, of innocence and temptation, of pastoral bliss and erotic sensuousness. Poets have borrowed the imagery of gardens and nature to evoke the blossoming of love

Gardens of the Senses

This medieval walled garden, in a 15th-century manuscript, presents an allegory of earthly delights recalling the biblical Eden.

Gardens of the Senses

(and its ephemerality) and the fertility of women, or simply to celebrate true

physical beauty. ("She opened her eyes," wrote D. H. Lawrence, "and green / They shone clear like flowers undone / For the first time, now for the first time seen.")

The atmosphere of a garden may be innocent or libidinous, pastoral or exotic. In the Judeo-Christian world-view, the idealized garden is the biblical one of chastity – Eden before the Fall, or the closed garden described in the Bible's Song of Songs: "a garden locked is my sister, my bride". The Song of Songs is itself a poetic evocation of the ancient walled gardens of Persia,

This French snuff box of 1749 (left) is decorated with exotic pinks – a symbol of betrothal, and a popular emblem on lovers' gifts.

An Indian miniature painting (below), ca. 1780, depicts a prince and his mistress in a garden setting.

Gardens of the Senses

This Renaissance painting (above) shows Flora, Roman goddess of flowers. She enjoyed perpetual spring in a garden of flowers and fruit, where the Graces twined garlands for their hair. Here, though, she reclines in a formal, Italianate-style setting.

and the Arabic word for paradise is *al-janna*, the garden. In secular art and poetry, the garden provides a scene for enchanting, perhaps overwhelming, the senses. The sexual imperative is manifest within the natural world: flowers, insects and birds reproduce themselves as part of a greater life force. Yet in the creation of an harmonious garden, wilder forces are restrained; order and sophistication have triumphed. In medieval courtly romances, such as *The Romance of the Rose*, the garden becomes an elegant battleground in the struggle for virtue.

The role of the garden in medieval romance is more than symbolic – it afforded welcome respite from the crowded communal life indoors. In the Renaissance, gardens became elaborately styled playgrounds, in which hidden water jets could surprise lovers – who in turn could surprise each other, as Jane Eyre later discovers when Rochester proposes to her in the garden at Thornfield. As modern lovers stroll through rose-walks, they are influenced by the weight of romantic allusion, as well as by the sights and scents around them.

FROM "SAKUNTALA"

Sensuous women

in summer love

weave

flower earrings

from fragile petals

of mimosa

while wild bees

kiss them gently.

5TH-CENTURY SANSKRIT PLAY

THE MYSTIC ROSE

 The pre-eminence of the rose as a love symbol goes back to antiquity when it was sacred to deities of love, especially the Greek goddess Aphrodite. Her priestesses wore white roses (emblems of virginity) and the paths of her shrines were strewn with rose petals. Together with its Eastern equivalent, the lotus, the flower became an enduring symbol of both human and spiritual desire, acquiring deeper mystical significance over time. The folded bud became a metaphor for the heart. The opening petals were an allegory, not only of birth and the source of life, but also of spiritual growth. In Tantric Buddhism, the fusion of sexual and spiritual aspiration is described as "the jewel in the lotus".

Christianity was slower to accept the rose as a comparable symbol of human and divine love, and it was only in the 13th century that an influential allegory

The Mystic Rose

While the white rose suggests youth and purity and the yellow one infidelity, the red rose represents passion.

of the mystic rose, *The Romance of the Rose*, appeared. This voluminous poem, begun by Guillaume de Lorris in 1236 and greatly lengthened by Jean de Meun 40 years later, depicts the art of love as a discipline beset with obstacles, requiring the slow development of self-knowledge. The young hero passionately desires to pick a rosebud (his beloved's innermost self) in the garden of love, but discovers that he must endure many frustrations before he can achieve this.

Many medieval depictions of courtly love are staged in gardens, which had Christian as well as sensual connotations.

The mystique of the rose is deeply ambiguous – by turns romantic, sacred and erotic. The rose symbolizes God's bounty, the glory of Nature itself, the beauty of the beloved and the promise of human love. An image of an earthly paradise, a rose garden may also represent the rosary – literally a garden of prayers to the Virgin Mary, the Rose of Heaven. Christ's heart, too, is a rose on fire with love, the thorns a symbol of his Passion.

The red rose is a highly charged image of sexual arousal, and of the vulva itself. Its scent, long the secret

Toward the end of *The Romance of the Rose*, the hero-poet, after undergoing a series of trials, attains the rose of his choice.

ingredient of perfumes, is a powerful aphrodisiac, as Cleopatra knew when she entertained Mark Antony in a room deep in rose petals. Little wonder that love can be declared by a single bloom.

THE KISS

Perhaps nowhere else is the poverty of a dictionary definition so exposed as in its description of a kiss: "a touch or pressure given with the lips in token of affection, greeting or reverence." The kiss of lovers, of course, is infinitely more than this. The erotic kiss is a psychological moment of enormous power which, for lovers, redefines all that went before. A kiss can appear to suspend time, to make the world dip out of sight, only to return transformed. We exchange the breath of life when we kiss lip to lip or nose to nose, as in the kisses of Maori and Eskimo people. The kiss is an act of union, and is recognized as such in religious and secular contexts.

In fairytales, the kiss changes all. It is the defining moment in many of these stories, which treat through metaphor the awakening of sexual consciousness.

The Kiss by Auguste Rodin is a remarkably sensitive and sensuous work, carved in marble.

The Kiss

Sleeping Beauty, Snow White and Wagner's sleeping Brunhilde are all awakened with a kiss from their long, pre-adolescent slumbers. For novelists depicting Western courtship, the first kiss of lovers may be a moment of exquisite, sometimes cataclysmic, intensity, heightened by delay. In Emily Brontë's *Wuthering Heights*,

Heathcliff waits four years to kiss Cathy, and then "neither spoke, nor loosed his hold for some five minutes, during which period he bestowed more kisses than ever he gave in his life before".

The kiss, so simple, yet so utterly transforming, is a uniquely human gesture that can celebrate tenderness and passion in a single, extraordinary moment.

O the water of love
that floods everything over, so that there is
nothing the eye sees that is not covered in.
There is no angle
the world can assume which the love in my
eye cannot make into a symbol of love.
Even the precise geometry
of his hand, when I gaze at it,
dissolves me into water and I flow away in
a flood of love.

ELIZABETH SMART (1913–86), FROM *By Grand Central Station I Sat Down and Wept*

THE NIGHT OF LOVE

The Night of Love

Lovers have always laid claim to the night as their own – a world apart, separate from the mundane complexities of the daylight hours. As reflected in love songs and poems across the centuries, night is perceived as an ally of lovers, and is part of their conspiracy of concealment. "The night was made for loving," wrote Byron, and Shakespeare's Juliet calls on the "love-producing night" to "spread thy close curtain". The lover in John Donne's famous poem "The Sunne Rising" tries to prolong the night by ordering away the sun: "Busie old foole, unruly Sunne / Why dost thou thus / Through windowes and through curtaines call on us? / Must to thy motions lovers' seasons run?"

Yet dawn must inevitably return, bringing with it, for lovers, the fear that

In this morning scene (above) a man is preparing to leave his lover, lying in glorious abandon on the bed. Clothes strewn hastily on the floor are further evidence of a night of passion.

Lovers (right), a linocut by John Buckland Wright, depicts a couple surrounded by the flames of their desire.

The Night of Love

the delights of the past night will prove to have been no more than an illusion. Women through history have feared, and found, that when the tasks of the day regain the man's attention, he will abandon them and withdraw into the 'rational' world.

The Arabian fairytale *The Thousand and One Nights* dramatizes these fears of male rejection. It tells the story of the all-powerful Sultan Schahriah, who has vowed to take a new bride every night, and to have each put to death at dawn, to prevent possible infidelity. However, the charming and intelligent heroine Scheherazade outwits him, surviving each night by telling a compelling story and promising to recount another the next night. After an onerous number of storytelling nights, she persuades the Sultan to revoke his decree and hail her as the liberator of women. This fairytale is an ancient call to arms by women against the purely sexual encounter, an enforced single night of love.

THE WANDERER

The idea that love is an amusing and pleasurable game of chase, conquest and skilful disengagement has existed for centuries in very different cultures. It remains a predominantly masculine concept, although the 'aggressors' have not always been men nor the 'victims' always women. Aspects of physiology as well as social traditions have contributed to the emergence of the wandering rake – an archetypal threat to those seeking an enduring love.

Jean Honoré Fragonard's painting *The Rape* illustrates the violence behind some supposed seductions carried out by literary rakes such as Don Juan.

Don Juan towers above other mythic seducers because he embodies several male fantasies on a heroic scale. Since his first appearance in Tirso de Molina's *The Rake of Seville* in 1630, Don Juan has epitomized the charming and profligate deceiver. Able to capture women's hearts almost at will, he nevertheless evades the tedious bonds of faithful love. Although his capacity to sustain relationships is non-existent, the Don's sense of adventure, curiosity, sexual appetite and physical energy are boundless. All this has made him particularly fascinating to male writers, for whom he is perhaps a metaphor for their own creative drive.

Dallying, by D. Miklos, shows a skilled seducer murmuring sweet nothings into a receptive feminine ear.

Psychotherapists who encounter "Don Juanism" in their patients classify it as an essentially childish and narcissistic condition. The motivations for it are many and varied, but include a boastful attempt to prove virility by purely sexual means, a basic incapacity to love or a present insecurity that refuses to limit future options. It is also a way of avoiding

Because of their inability to form lasting relationships, wandering lovers are often alone in the end.

The Wanderer

commitment to a long-term partner who might find weaknesses behind superficial bravado. However, analysis of the somewhat pathetic philanderers of reality shows them to be in strong contrast to the engaging Don Juan in his literary, dramatic and operatic manifestations.

Stendhal, whose work displays his great sensitivity for women, dismissed the Don as "a dishonest trader who takes but never pays". Not surprisingly, Byron took another view. He perceived an attractive adventurer, whose wish to make love to all women rather than just one rendered him a tireless, devoted worshipper at the shrine of the Eternal Feminine. Molière's Don Juan mockingly stresses the generosity of his indiscriminate attachments. "I am fond of freedom in love ... As soon as a beautiful face asks me for my heart, I would give them all if I had 10,000 hearts." In Mozart's opera *Don Giovanni*, the protagonist is portrayed as a romantic free spirit, whose libertine activities challenge far more than sexual conventions. A charming rebel who is opposed to all limits, human or divine, his defiant courage is overborne at last by a greater, supernatural authority.

Don Juan could not have become a hero without being refreshingly honest about himself. Self-confessed rakes through history have freely admitted to enjoying obstacles as part of the hunt for love. The thrill of encountering a new personality and body fuses with the discovery of a new self through another's eyes. As well as the prestige of conquest, wanderers are able to recapture time and again the initial passions of love.

A successful philanderer is almost by definition extremely attractive. Skilled in charming others, presenting an irresistible challenge, rakes have always offered a dangerous excitement that transforms an ordinary love affair. Whatever the deplorable morality of the wanderers' conduct, and the emotional chaos that they may cause, they appear never lacking in attentive lovers.

The Wanderer

The Mirrored Self

In this Aubrey Beardsley illustration entitled *The Mirror of Love*, the heart-shaped glass reflects an image of Eros, the god of love.

THE MIRRORED SELF

*To love oneself
is the beginning of a lifelong romance.*

OSCAR WILDE (1854–1900)

To some extent, we all resemble Narcissus in Ovid's famous myth – the beautiful youth who pined and died of unrequited love for his own reflection in a pool. With the exception of a partner whom we truly love, nobody is more important to us than ourselves.

The reason Ovid gave for the fate of Narcissus is psychologically penetrating. He had spurned any other love and was punished for it by Nemesis, who heard the cry of a nymph he had rejected: "So may he himself fall in love, so may he himself not be able to possess his beloved!" In other words, self-love can be so strong that we are unable to love anyone else; narcissism is self-destructive.

Narcissism is an element in all human love. It is part of our longing for union with another being, in which identities become subsumed. "I am Heathcliff!" cries the despairing Catherine Earnshaw in Emily Brontë's *Wuthering Heights*, expressing a feeling that most true lovers have experienced. The sense of loving aspects of one-self as they are perceived by a lover may be particularly acute in same-sex relationships, where the adored object is in some ways a mirror image. Narcissus, totally enraptured by his own youthful beauty, is often held to be an archetype of gay male love. The psychoanalyst Sigmund Freud believed that homosexual relationships derived in part from a search for an idealized version of the ego, or the desire to repossess a youthful self. Accepting a degree of narcissism seems

> THE RAIN PALACE
> *I have built for you a rain palace*
> *Of alabaster columns and rock crystal*
> *So that a thousand mirrors shall tell me*
> *How ever more beautifully for me*
> *you change.*
>
> YVAN GOLL,
> TRS FROM THE GERMAN
> BY MICHAEL HAMBURGER

The Mirrored Self

to be an essential part of loving. Yet it can be a subject for comedy, as in Shakespeare's *Much Ado About Nothing*, where the apparently antagonistic Beatrice and Benedick switch from taunting to loving each other the moment that they hear the other adores them. The beloved object becomes a reflection of our own attractiveness. In paintings, Venus is often portrayed gazing into a mirror, the traditional emblem of love, beauty and happiness. The broken mirror, by contrast, has always symbolized bad luck in love – possibly connected to the ancient belief that the reflection was a twin soul. Narcissus, whose self-love was fatally exclusive, suffered anguish when his reflection broke as he attempted to grasp it in the waters of the pool.

This 16th-century painting of Narcissus shows the beautiful youth gazing at his own reflection in a pool. The love of an image is ultimately unrewarding, and Narcissus pines away. As he dies he is transformed into the delicate narcissus flower.

The Devourer

The Devourer

"Heaven has no rage, like love to hatred turned, / Nor hell a fury, like a woman scorned," wrote William Congreve at the turn of the 17th century. He expressed a deep-seated and enduring male fear that love can unleash uncontrollable and destructive emotions in women. Mythology and folklore have created a gallery of frightening women, governed by jealousy and revenge.

Anthony Sandys' painting *Love's Shadow* shows a vengeful-looking woman devouring a posy of flowers, possibly given to her by a lover.

One explanation for this pervasive archetype is its connection with a terrifying mother figure, invested with the power to create and destroy. These conflicting attributes have been fused in female goddesses for centuries, reflecting the two principles of sex and death on which the natural world depends. The Hindu goddess Devi reveals this dual role in her incarnations as benign Parvati and ferocious Kali. The latter's manifestation as the "dark one", garlanded with skulls and engulfing enemies in a cavernous mouth, emphasizes the sexual aspect of her relentless, terrifying authority.

The dreadful female devourer is also integral to Western religious traditions. Many biblical stories feature women who destroy or emasculate men. Judith cuts off the head of the enemy general Holofernes while he sleeps in her arms. Samson's lover Delilah coaxes from him

LIKE GULLIVER

Like Gulliver pulling a hundred ships,
I draw you, my lovers, to the shore,
clumsy, in all colours, cunning with your
tiny swords and shooting from the hips.

Like Gulliver I spare you, even though
you hit my skull cruelly and hope it breaks.
I laugh at you through strings and snakes
of blood, my furious lovers with your
tiny bows.

NINA CASSIAN (1924–),
TRS FROM THE ROMANIAN BY
WILLIS BARNSTONE AND MATEI CALINESCU

the secret of his superhuman strength – his hair – and tells his enemies to cut it while he sleeps.

Greek mythology contains a variety of avenging, destructive women, who are epitomized by the terrible Furies. Known euphemistically as the Eumenides, or "Kindly Ones", they hound their prey for years to remind them of their guilt. A woman was thought to pose the greatest threat to a man when he was off-guard and alone – a metaphor for male emotional vulnerability outside the rational world. For example, when the king of Argos, Agamemnon, returns home safely after the Trojan Wars, his treacherous queen, Clytemnestra, enmeshes him in a net and murders him.

The image of the devourer seems to feed upon a wide range of male fears. On one level the archetype embodies male anxieties about the excessive demands of female love, and a corresponding inability to recognize the depths of a woman's passion.

A sense of enchantment runs throughout Keats' poem of betrayed love, *La Belle Dame sans Merci*, in which a knight is seduced by a lady in the woods. He falls into a troubled sleep and when he wakes she has gone.

The Devourer

THE TEMPTRESS

The Temptress

The serpent in the Garden of Eden persuades Eve to offer Adam the forbidden fruit, making her Christianity's first temptress.

From a modern viewpoint, Adam's part in the Fall seems more duplicitous than Eve's. He ate the forbidden fruit that she offered him, and then blamed his wife for his own wrongdoing. However, history forgave his weakness and his disloyalty – and proceeded to confuse the woman with the serpent. The archetype of the temptress was thus established – a dangerous and amoral seducer of men.

Bizet's Carmen is one of the most dramatic examples of a woman who takes the initiative in love. She is a dark, mysterious, fiery creature who whirls the fascinated José from the arms of his kindly, dull local sweetheart, only to drop him at whim for a famous bullfighter. Such male arbitrariness cannot be tolerated in a woman and Carmen, who is like a feminine version of Don

Until the 20th century, flowing locks were seen as provocative and unruly in most societies. This 18th-century Indian miniature shows a woman dressing her hair.

Juan in her free sensuality, pays for her sexual independence with her life.

Men's traditional excuse for falling in love with a temptress is that she deploys supernatural powers. In Homer's poem *The Odyssey*, for example, the beautiful island sorceress Circe ensnared even the wily Odysseus, returning home from the wars of Troy. In mythology, the island with its temptress is often a metaphor for irresponsible pleasure – a true sensual haven, isolated from the world. The final threat – or promise – is that this idyll could become permanent: on another island, the nymph Calypso had it in her gift to offer Odysseus immortality.

The Temptress

THE BROKEN VOW

The Broken Vow

In *Broken Vows*, a painting by P. H. Calderon, a distraught woman over-hears her lover flirting with another.

Novels of the 19th century are littered with women jilted at the altar, or earlier, by seducers who never intended to keep their vows. Underlying these scenes was the fear of the betrayal of love within marriage itself. The whole literature of love tells us that its vows are not like other promises. They are emotional, not rational, and based on the impulses of the heart – a notoriously unreliable organ.

All true lovers deny the power of time to erode their feelings. For them, the boast of Enobarbus in Shakespeare's *Antony and Cleopatra* carries absolute conviction: "Age cannot wither her, nor custom stale / Her infinite variety." However, in literature – and often in life – the joyous comedy of falling in love is matched by the tragedy of falling out of it.

Often a third party simply provides the catalyst for a failing relationship, yet adultery causes great bitterness. One of the paradoxes of love is that disloyalty to an old love may seem acceptable if it is for the sake of a new. The concept of a noble betrayal infuses the medieval tradition of courtly love, which clearly distinguishes between the vows of love and those of marriage. Yet what is seldom absent from any of these stories is the pervasive, insidious effect of guilt – the inescapable result of the broken vow.

The Broken Vow

In the 16th-century French painting *Woman Between Two Ages of Man*, a woman removes the glasses from her elderly husband, thus blinding him to her adultery with a handsome young lover.

The Broken Vow

THE QUARREL

Seemingly foolish and often explosive, the lovers' quarrel is an ancient rite for couples, a way of reiterating and recharging the love that they are in the midst of denying. "Lovers' quarrels," wrote the Roman playwright Terence, "are the renewal of love." The quarrel is flirtation in disguise, a sexually charged, verbal tussle which allows lovers to recreate the beginning of their love. "When with unkindness our love at a stand is / And both have punish'd ourselves with the pain, / Ah what a pleasure the touch of her hand is, / Ah what a pleasure to press it again," sighed John Dryden. At the end of Jane Austen's insightful novel *Pride and Prejudice*, Elizabeth Bennett actually promises to argue with Mr Darcy when married: "... it belongs to me to find occasions for teasing and quarrelling with you as often as may be."

Literature relishes the conflicts of magnificently noisy couples, for example

the skirmishes of Stella and Stanley in Tennessee Williams' play *A Streetcar Named Desire* and the passionate taunts of Shakespeare's Antony and Cleopatra. Their quarrels contain an absurdity familiar to everyone who has found in the burnt dinner a peg on which to hang the real issue: is love still there?

The body language of the woman in Emma Turpin's *The Talking Garden* suggests that she is distancing herself from her lover, perhaps after a quarrel.

The Quarrel

Perhaps because young love is expected to blow hot and cold, age tends to dismiss its quarrels as tiffs. However, tiffs in a relationship are rarely outgrown. Lovers continue to ambush each other with arguments into old age, possibly as a challenge to the tedium of perpetual harmony. This complex manoeuvring is often essential to the survival of love itself. As Alain de Botton writes in his *Essays on Love*, we mistakenly cling "to the idea of a hermetic division between love and non-love, one that should be crossed only twice, at the beginning and end of a relationship – rather than commuted across daily, or hourly. There is an impulse to split love and hate apart, rather than to see them as legitimate responses to the many sides of a single person."

The complex and often irrational fluctuation of our feelings promotes arguments in most close relationships. However, it is the intensity of our

emotional preoccupation with a partner that gives such quarrels a much deeper, lasting significance. It may suddenly expose any fragility in a relationship with brutal clarity, startling both parties with the violence of the feelings that are revealed. Yet no affair of the heart can endure without the ability to weather an argument and to savour reconciliation – and love itself may well emerge stronger as a consequence.

The Quarrel

In Dudley Hardy's *A Slight Difference of Opinion*, a woman ignores her lover as he leaves.

THE PARTING

Sleeplessness is common when we are separated from the one we love. In this Indian miniature, a lady is waiting through the night for her lover to return.

The anguish of lovers who cannot be together has been the inspiration for some of the world's most enduring literature on love. The anonymous 16th-century poem, "Western Wind", provides a powerful emotional charge: "Western wind, when will thou blow, / The small rain down can rain? / Christ, if my love were in my arms / And I in my bed again!" An 8th-century Chinese poem, "The River-Merchant's Wife: A Letter", describes a young wife who feels such longing for her absent husband that even the sight of paired butterflies is a source of pain: "They hurt me. I grow older."

Schopenhauer, the philosopher, wrote that "every parting gives a foretaste of death", a perception particularly true of wartime partings, which are filled with anticipatory dread. "How long ago Hector took off his plume / Not wanting that his little son should cry / Then kisses his sad Andromache goodbye – / And now we

three in Euston waiting-room." Frances Cornford's sober poem recognizes the timelessness of such anguished farewells, and, in the allusion to the fated Trojan prince Hector and his widow, the heroism of those who have to endure them.

Passionate good-byes, such as the one captured in this collage by Amy Shuckburgh, have long been one of the staples of film-makers.

THE LOVE-DEATH

Romantic love has always been aware of its own fragility. As heightened emotion brings us to the extremes of existence, it also increases our consciousness of death. The hope that love may endure after death finds expression in the myths and artefacts of

The story of Tristan and Isolde is one of the most enduring medieval romances. Their love was aroused by a magic potion – they eventually died as a consequence of their forbidden passion.

many diverse cultures. The often-told story of Orpheus, who sought to rescue his beloved Eurydice from Hades, seems to embody a common human resistance to the idea that death must inevitably divide lovers. Joint tombs date from antiquity, and tokens such as the "bracelet of bright haire" that John Donne imagines tied around his arm after death symbolize the desire for lasting union. The poignancy of such gestures, and of love itself, lies in the contrast between what we know rationally and feel emotionally. We recognize mortality, but refuse to accept the extinguishing of emotions that once seemed infinite.

The 19th century enjoyed a romantic obsession with death, and the question of whether love could outlast it. A Christian religious faith offered hope to Elizabeth Barrett Browning, who wrote to her husband Robert: "I love thee with the breath / Smiles, tears, of all my life! – and, if God choose / I shall but love thee better after death."

Lovers who opt to die together rather

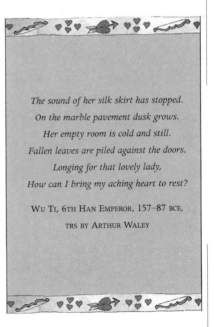

The sound of her silk skirt has stopped.
On the marble pavement dusk grows.
Her empty room is cold and still.
Fallen leaves are piled against the doors.
Longing for that lovely lady,
How can I bring my aching heart to rest?

WU TI, 6TH HAN EMPEROR, 157–87 BCE,
TRS BY ARTHUR WALEY

The Love-Death

235

The Love-Death

than survive alone have featured in tragic drama and opera for centuries. Often their decision is based on a tragic misunderstanding, as in the deaths of Shakespeare's Romeo and Juliet or the lovers of Ovid's tale of Pyramus and Thisbe. The idea of the love-death is perfected in the Wagnerian *Liebestod* of Tristan and Isolde. The composer translated the medieval story of guilt-ridden love into an opera that celebrates the triumph of true love over death. As Tristan dies, Isolde – by a sheer effort of will – collapses dead over his body. The lovers achieve a union in death that, paradoxically, could never have been sustained in life.

The love-death theme expresses the emotional truth that life may seem insupportable without the loved one. Puccini's heroine Tosca, for example, chooses to leap to her death after realizing that her lover, Cavaradossi, has been executed.

Although few people actually die of love, the point of the archetype is that innumerable parted lovers have longed

This work by Alessandro Varotari depicts the story of Orpheus and his wife Eurydice. When Eurydice died, Orpheus sought her in Hades. He failed to win her back and was later killed by a band of women who were tired of his grieving.

to die. There is also a deep-seated horror of letting an adored Other go into the afterworld alone. The desire to go hand-in-hand is irrational – but so are many impulses of passionate love.

The Love-Death

THE ONE AND ONLY

For centuries, the idea of exclusivity has held great emotional appeal for romantic love. Our different relationships in the real world prove that how we love, and whom, may alter over time. Yet the belief that we can truly love only once keeps a pervasive hold on the human imagination.

The concept of a "one and only" love is very ancient. It forms the central theme of the beautiful Song of Songs, in the Old Testament of the Bible. The book is unique and so mysterious that scholars have never been able to agree on who wrote it or what it means. It seems to be a dialogue between a king (supposedly Solomon) and a lovely Shulamite girl who longs to leave his harem to be reunited with her adored shepherd. The power and sweetness of its poetry insist that romantic love can never be divided, but must be devoted to one single other soul.

The literature of love has celebrated this idea ever since. Yet our emotions remain complex, elusive and fluid – what and whom we love, what we feel and what we find lovable are all subject to change over time.

F. Scott Fitzgerald's poignant and powerful novel *The Great Gatsby* describes its hero's failure to understand this. Jay Gatsby's first love, Daisy, has married a rich man, and Jay spends years making himself even richer before he attempts, fatally, to replay the idealized romance of his youth. Only Nick, the narrator, realizes the ephemerality of Gatsby's illusions: "He had come a long way to this blue lawn, and his dream must have seemed so close that he could hardly fail to grasp it. He did not know that it was already behind him, somewhere back in that vast obscurity beyond the city, where the dark fields of the republic rolled on under the night."

The One and Only

The One and Only

Committing
ourselves to one
person radically
changes the
way we view
our lives. In
this painting
by Emma Turpin
a bride finds
herself in a new
and strange land.

THE WORLD WELL LOST

This 14th-century miniature depicts the lovers Peter Abélard and his pupil Héloïse. The couple are clearly still fascinated by each another, despite their religious orders and the cruelty they have both suffered for their love.

The bittersweetness of love is so finely balanced that we cannot always be sure that the happiness it brings will out-weigh the pain. The power in the idea of a world well lost for love derives from the real-life exemplars. For the medieval world it was epitomized by the French lovers Abélard and Héloïse.

Peter Abélard, a great 12th-century theologian, plunged into a passionate, illicit love affair with his pupil, Héloïse.

She bore his child, after which Abélard was emasculated by her vindictive uncle. From the convent which she entered, Héloïse wrote hundreds of letters to Abélard. "Not piety, only an order from you has delivered me up so young to the rigours of monastic life,"

The World Well Lost

FROM "THE RUBÁIYÁT
OF OMAR KHAYYÁM"

Alas, that Spring should vanish with the Rose!
That Youth's sweet-scented Manuscript
should close!
The Nightingale that in the Branches sang,
Ah, whence, and whither flown again,
who knows!

Ah Love! could thou and I with Fate conspire
To grasp this sorry Scheme of Things entire,
Would not we shatter it to bits – and then
Re-mould it nearer to the Heart's Desire!

EDWARD FITZGERALD (1809–83)

she wrote. "God knows, I would not have hesitated to follow you or go before you into Hell if you had ordered me to do so." Her life was dedicated to the love that she continued to feel for Abélard. When he died, his body was brought to Héloïse's convent for burial.

The strains inherent in putting love before everything else were explored by the Russian writer Leo Tolstoy in his novel *Anna Karenina*. Anna is a beautiful woman whose dull married life is transformed by her passion for an attractive young officer, Count Vronsky. In order to be with her lover, Anna must abandon her adored child. Before long, Vronsky, who has given up his army career for Anna, begins to feel the unbearable pressure of his obligation to maintain love at the heightened level that justified these huge sacrifices. In depicting the affair's fatal outcome, Tolstoy reminds us that ultimately lovers cannot forget the real world in which they have to live.

The World Well Lost

This late 18th-century painting from Rajasthan shows two lovers lying on a couch under a canopy. At such moments the cares of the real world vanish or become, for a time at least, insignificant.

BIBLIOGRAPHY

Barnstone, A. and W. (eds) *A Book of Women Poets*. New York: Schocken Books, 1980.

Bergmann, M. S. *The Anatomy of Loving*. New York: Columbia University Press, 1987.

Boase, R. *The Origin and Meaning of Courtly Love*. Manchester: Manchester University Press, 1977.

Charter, R. (ed.) *A History of Private Life*. Cambridge, Mass.: Harvard University Press, 1987.

Clayton, J. *Romantic Vision and the Novel*. Cambridge: Cambridge University Press, 1987.

De Botton, A. *The Romantic Movement*. London: Macmillan, 1994.

de la Mare, W. *Love (anthology)*. London: Faber, 1943.

Epton, N. *Love and the French*. London: Cassell, 1959.

Epton, N. *Love and the Spanish*. London: Cassell, 1961.

Fuller, J. (ed.) *The Chatto Book of Love Poetry*. London: Chatto & Windus, 1990.

Fromm, E. *The Art of Loving*. London: Allen & Unwin, 1957.

Gunn, A. M. F. *The Mirror of Love*. Lubbock: Texas Technical Press, 1952.

Hagstrum, J. H. *The Romantic Body*. Knoxville: University of Tennessee Press, 1986.

Hilton, T. *Keats and His World*. London: Thames & Hudson, 1971.

Huot, S. *The Romance of the Rose*. Cambridge: Cambridge University Press, 1993.

Kennedy, B. *Knighthood in the Morte d'Arthur*. Cambridge: D. S. Brewer, 1985.

Lilar, S. *Aspects of Love*. London: Thames & Hudson trs by Jonathan Griffin, 1965.

Lockridge, L. S. *The Ethics of Romanticism*. Cambridge: Cambridge University Press, 1989.

Lystra, K. *Searching the Heart*. New York: Oxford University Press, 1989.

Morphod, M. P. O. and Lenardon, R. J., *Classical Mythology*. White Plains, New York: Longman, 1995.

O'Brien, E. *Some Irish Loving*. London: Weidenfeld & Nicholson, 1979.

Owen, D. (compiler) *Seven Ages: Poetry for a Lifetime*. London: Michael Joseph, 1992.

Stallworthy, J. (ed.) *The Penguin Book of Love Poetry*. London: Allen Lane, 1973.

Stendhal, *Love*. London: Merlin Press translation, 1957.

Tergit, G. *Flowers through the Ages*. London: Oswald Wolff, 1961.

Turner, J. *Love Letters, 975–1944*. London: Cassell, 1969.

Zeldin, T. *An Intimate History of Humanity*. London: Sinclair-Stevenson, 1994.

INDEX

Index

Index

TEXT ACKNOWLEDGMENTS

The author and publishers would like to thank the following for permission to reproduce their copyright material. Every care has been taken to trace copyright owners, but if we have omitted anyone we apologize and will, if informed, make corrections in any future edition.

Page 23 extract from "Adultery" by Thom Gunn from *The Passages of Joy*, reprinted by permission of Faber and Faber Ltd, London, and from *The Complete Poems* by Randall Jarrell. Copyright © 1969, renewed 1997 by Mary von S. Jarrell. Reprinted by permission of Farrar Straus & Giroux, LLC., New York; **29** "I am yours, you are mine" by Frau Ava translated by Willis Barnstone from *A Book of Woman Poets from Antiquity to Now*, by Willis Barnstone and Aliki Barnstone, copyright © 1980 by Schocken Books, a division of Random House, Inc., used by permission of Schocken Books, a division of Random House, Inc.; **40** "At Parting" by Anne Ridler from *Collected Poems*, reprinted by permission of Carcanet Press Ltd; **62** "The Saddest Lines" by Pablo Neruda from *Selected Poems*, published by Jonathan Cape, reprinted by permission of The Random House Group; **83** "When I Praise" by W.H. Davies from *The Collected Poems of W.H. Davies* published by Jonathan Cape, reprinted by permission of Mrs H.M. Davies Will Trust, courtesy Dee & Griffin, Gloucester; **91** "Meslanges, 2, VI" by Ronsard, translated by Laurence Kitchen from *Love Sonnets of the Renaissance*, reprinted by permission of Forest Books; **120** extract from "Strawberries" by Edwin Morgan, reprinted by permission of Carcanet Press Ltd; **126** "They who are near to me" by Rabindranath Tagore from *The Collected Poems and Plays of Rabindranath Tagore*, reprinted by permission of Macmillan General Books, London and with permission of Scribner, an imprint of Simon & Schuster Adult Publishing Group, New York, copyright © 1937 by Macmillan Publishing Company: copyright renewed © 1965; **131** extract from "One Perfect Rose" by Dorothy Parker from *The Collected Dorothy Parker*, reprinted by permission of Gerald Duckworth & Co. Ltd, London and from *Dorothy Parker: Complete Poems* by Dorothy Parker, © 1999 by The National Association for the Advancement of Colored People. Used by permission of Penguin, a division of Penguin Group (USA) Inc.; **153** extract from "The Bride" by Bella Akhmadulina translated by Stephen Stepanchev from *A Book of Woman Poets from Antiquity to Now*, reprinted by permission of Schocken Books; **175** "The Three-Faced" by Robert Graves from *Poems About Love*, reprinted by permission of Carcanet Press Ltd; **182** extract from "Leda and the Swan" by W. B. Yeats from *The Collected Works of W. B. Yeats, Volume 1: The Poems, Revised*, edited by Richard J. Finneran, reprinted by permission of A.P. Watt Ltd, London, on behalf of Michael Yeats, and with permission of Scribner, an imprint of Simon & Schuster Adult Publishing Group, New York, copyright © 1928 by Macmillan Publishing Company, copyright renewed © 1956 by Georgie Yeats; **192** extract from "Green Song" by Edith Sitwell from *Collected Poems*, published by Sinclair-Stevenson, reprinted by permission of David Higham Associates; **205** extract from *By Grand Central Station I Sat Down and Wept* by Elizabeth Smart, reprinted by permission of The Estate of Elizabeth Smart and HarperCollins Publishers Ltd; **215** "The Rain Palace" by Yvan Goll translated by Michael Hamburger from *German Poetry 1910–1975*, published by Carcanet Press Ltd, translation © Michael Hamburger; **219** "Like Gulliver" by Nina Cassian translated by Willis Barnstone and Matei Calinescu from *A Book of Woman Poets from Antiquity to Now* by Willis Barnstone and Aliki Barnstone, copyright © 1980 by Schocken Books, a division of Random House, Inc., used by permission of Schocken Books, a division of Random House, Inc.; **230** extract from *Essays in Love* by Alain de Botton, reprinted by permission of Picador/Macmillan General Books, London; **232–233** extract from "Parting in Wartime" by Frances Cornford from *Frances Cornford Collected Poems*, published by Cresset Press, reprinted by permission of the Trustees of Frances Crofts Cornford Deceased Will Trust; **235** "The sound of her silk skirt has stopped" by Wu Ti translated by Arthur Waley, from *A Hundred and Seventy Chinese Poems* reprinted by kind permission of Constable & Robinson Ltd and by permission of The Arthur Waley Estate.

PICTURE ACKNOWLEDGMENTS

The author and publishers would like to thank the following people, museums and photographic libraries for permission to reproduce their material. Every care has been taken to trace copyright owners. However, if we have omitted anyone we apologize and will, if informed, make corrections in any future edition.

Key:

AA   Art Archive, London
BAL   Bridgeman Art Library, London

Page 1 British Library, London (BAL); **2** © Emma Turpin; **8** © Emma Turpin; **10–11** © Celia Birtwell, London; **12** Private Collection (BAL); **13** Musée Cluny, Paris (BAL); **14** Louvre, Paris (BAL); **15** Borghese Gallery, Rome (AKG, London); **16** Victoria & Albert Museum, London (BAL); **19** Private Collection (BAL); **20** British Library, London (BAL); **21** left Private Collection; **21** right Wolseley Fine Arts, London © Courtesy of the Estate of Eric Gill, Bridgeman Art Library; **22** © Emma Turpin; **24** left and **25** right Rose Castle, Cumbria (BAL); **24** right Museo Diocesano de Solsona Lerida (BAL); **26** Victoria & Albert Museum, London (AA); **27** Private Collection (BAL); **30** right Victoria & Albert Museum, London (BAL); **31** Private Collection (BAL); **32** British Museum. London; **33** Fitzwilliam Museum, University of Cambridge (BAL); **34** Private Collection (Christie's Images); **35** Prado, Madrid (AKG, London); **36** British Library, London (BAL); **37** © Emma Turpin; **38** Bibliothèque Nationale, Paris (BAL); **41** © Thurston Hopkins/Portfolio Ltd, London; **42–43** © Thurston Hopkins/Portfolio Ltd, London; **44** above British Library, London (BAL); **45** Musée Condé, Chantilly (AKG, London/Erich Lessing); **44**, **45** and **46** details Musée Mobilier National, Paris (BAL); **46** Louvre, Paris (AKG, London/Erich Lessing); **47** above Private Collection; **47** below National Gallery, London; **48** © Emma Turpin; **49** Kunsthistorisches Museum, Vienna (BAL); **51** Museo Civico, Ascoli Piceno (AA); **52–53** National Gallery, Budapest (AA); **56** Private Collection; **56–57** Borough of Southwark, London (BAL); **58** University of Liverpool Art Gallery (BAL); **59** Wolsley Fine Arts, London © Courtesy of the Estate of Eric Gill, Bridgeman Art Library; **60–61** © Emma Turpin; **63** Wolseley Fine Arts, London © Courtesy of the Estate of Eric Gill, Bridgeman Art Library; **64–65** © Trevor Watson/Portfolio Ltd, London; **66–67** © Emma Turpin; **68** Victoria & Albert Museum, London (AKG, London); **71** The Wallace

Collection, London (BAL); **72** Wolverhampton Art Gallery (BAL); **74** below Victoria & Albert Museum, London (BAL); **74** above and **77** National Gallery, London; **75** © Emma Turpin; **76** Roy Miles Gallery, London (BAL); **78** National Gallery, London; **79** Private Collection (David Lavender); **81** Musée Cluny, Paris (BAL); **83** Musée Bonnat, Bayonne (AA); **84** Lutherhalle, Wittenberg (AKG, London); **86** Fine Art Society, London (BAL); **87** Private Collection (AA); **89** © Roderick A. Field/Portfolio Ltd, London; **90–91** © Thurston Hopkins/Portfolio Ltd, London; **92** Private Collection (BAL); **93** Musée Condé, Chantilly (BAL); **95** Private Collection (AA); **96** Christopher Wood Gallery, London (BAL); **97** Ca' Rezzonico, Venice (AA); **98** above Palazzo Ducale, Mantua (BAL); **98** below Musée d'Orsay, Paris (AA); **100** Belvedere Galerie, Vienna (AKG, London); **101** Bibliothèque Nationale, Paris (BAL); **102–103** © Emma Turpin; **104** Wolseley Fine Arts, London © Courtesy of the Estate of Eric Gill, Bridgeman Art Library; **106–107** © Emma Turpin; **108** Towneley Collection, British Museum, London (AKG, London); **110–111** © Emma Turpin; **113** Ca' Rezzonico, Venice (AA); **114** Georgian State Picture Gallery, Tbilisi (BAL); **115** Private Collection (BAL); **116** above and **117** below Victoria & Albert Museum, London (BAL); **116** below Victoria & Albert Museum, London (AA); **117** above Musée des Beaux-Arts, Lille (BAL); **119** Ca' Rezzonico, Venice (AA); **120** British Library, London (AA); **121** above and below Museo de America, Madrid (BAL); **122–123** Private Collection (JB Archive, London); **125** above Private Collection (AA); **125** below National Gallery of Ireland, Dublin (BAL); **127** Private Collection (BAL) © Estate of Stanley Spencer, 2004. All Rights Reserved, DACS; **128** above Private Collection (DBP Archive); **128** below Christie's, London (BAL); **129** above Private Collection (AA); **129** below Private Collection; **130** Private Collection (BAL); **131** © Gill Orsman, London; **132–133** Victoria & Albert Museum, London (BAL); **134** above Private Collection; **134** below © Emma Turpin; **135** above National Museum of American Art, Washington D.C. (BAL); **135** below Private Collection (Christie's Images, London); **136** Private Collection (David Lavender); **137** Private Collection; **139** © Richard McConnell, London; **140–141** © Caroline Arber/Portfolio Ltd, London; **142** above Bibliothèque Nationale, Paris (BAL); **142** below Private Collection (AKG, London); **143** Prado, Madrid (AA); **145** Private Collection (AKG, London); **146–147** Phillips Fine Art Auctioneers, London (BAL); **149** details Private Collection (DBP

Picture Acknowledgments

Archive); **149** Private Collection (BAL); **150** Prado, Madrid (AA); **151** National Gallery, London (BAL); **152** Fitzwilliam Museum, University of Cambridge (BAL); **153** Wolseley Fine Art, London © Courtesy of the Estate of Eric Gill, Bridgeman Art Library; **154–155** Private Collection (BAL); **156–157** © Emma Turpin; **158** National Gallery, London; **160** Duke of Sutherland Collection, National Gallery of Scotland (BAL); **161** Freud Museum, London (BAL); **162–163** Uffizi, Florence (AKG, London); **165** Museum der Bildenden Kunste, Leipzig (AKG, London); **167** Osterreichische Galerie, Vienna (BAL); **168** above Maas Gallery, London (BAL); **168** below Private Collection (BAL); **170** Kunsthistorisches Museum, Vienna (BAL); **172** British Library, London (BAL); **173** Musée d'Orsay, Paris (AA); **174** Victoria & Albert Museum, London (BAL); **176** Private Collection (AA); **177** Whitford & Hughes, London (BAL); **178** Bibliothèque Nationale, Paris (BAL); **179** above Musée de Cluny (AKG, London); **181** above Louvre, Paris (BAL); **181** below Victoria & Albert Museum, London (BAL); **183** Louvre, Paris (BAL); **185** Forbes Magazine Collection, London (BAL); **184** Roy Miles Gallery, London (BAL); **188–189** © Emma Turpin; **190** British Library, London (BAL); **191** above Kobal Collection, London; **191** below Bibliothèque Nationale, Paris (BAL); **193** National Gallery, London (BAL); **195** Bibliothèque Nationale, Paris (AKG, London); **196** above Christie's, London (BAL); **196** below Private Collection (BAL); **197** National Museum, Stockholm (BAL); **200** © Gill Orsman, London; **201** Musée Condé, Chantilly (BAL); **202** British Library, London (BAL); **203** Musée Rodin, Paris (AKG, London); **204** Taylor Gallery, London (BAL); **206** Musée des Beaux-Arts, Bordeaux (BAL); **207** Wolseley Fine Arts, London © The Heirs of John Buckland Wright; **209** Louvre, Paris (AKG, London); **210** National Gallery of Hungarian Art, Budapest (AA); **211** © Emma Turpin; **214** Victoria & Albert Museum, London (BAL); **216** City of Bristol Museum & Art Gallery (BAL); **218** Forbes Magazine Collection, London (BAL); **220** Hessisches Landesmuseum, Darmstadt (BAL); **222** Private Collection; **223** Private Collection (BAL); **224** Tate Gallery, London (AA); **226–227** Prado, Madrid (BAL); **229** © Emma Turpin; **230–231** Fine-Lines, Warwickshire (BAL); **239** © Emma Turpin; **232** Victoria & Albert Museum, London (BAL); **233** © Amy Shuckburgh, London; **234** British Library, London (BAL); **237** Accademia, Venice (BAL); **241–242** © Emma Turpin; **242** Musée Condé, Chantilly (BAL); **244–5** Private Collection (BAL).